Plan your home

BATHROOMS

José Manser

Studio Vista

Cover photograph
Leafy green and blue bathroom designed by Royal
Ballet dancer Petrus Bosman for his London home.
(*Courtesy of Ideal Home*)

© 1969 José Manser
Published 1969 by Studio Vista Limited
Blue Star House, Highgate Hill, London N19
Set in 9D on 11pt Univers
Printed and bound in Holland by
Drukkerij Reclame N.V.
SBN 289 79680 6 (paperback)
    289 79681 4 (hardbound)

Contents

Introduction

When we are barely awake, freezing cold or filthy dirty, the place for which we are most likely to head is the bathroom. Man, woman and child, it is a room we all have to use, often when we are at low ebb and in need of comfort. Yet, unlike the kitchen, which is traditionally woman's territory and therefore perhaps more stridently demanding of attention, the bathroom in many houses tends to have been passed over, even during an orgy of rehabilitation and decoration. The care, thought and imagination (cash too) which are lavished on other parts of the house never seem to converge on the bathroom. This is a pity. There have in recent years been developments, both technical and decorative, which can help to make bathrooms the warm, comfortable and attractive places they should be. Statistics tell us we are getting cleaner every year, certainly more people have more bathrooms every year, so we might just as well do all this washing against a good-looking and convenient background.

If it is properly designed, a bathroom can be fairly easy to keep clean. A variety of materials can be used to line the walls, from laminated plastic to plastic coated wallpaper, as well as tiles which no longer have the strictly clinical connotations of the past. Even if your house is not centrally heated it is possible, in fact essential, to have a warm bathroom, and there are inexpensive—and safe—ways of achieving local heat. Condensation can be avoided, floors can be soft and comforting or hard and hygienic, lights and lighting can be exactly as required. I shall discuss all these aspects of the bathroom in detail later in the book, but the first and most important thing to consider is the initial planning.

Baths, lavatories and washbasins are the most expensive items in a bathroom: installing them, unless you do it yourself, will not be cheap, and changing either the actual goods or the layout at a later stage is a costly procedure. So it is important to be quite sure of your needs at the planning stage. Planning is also important because it can give or deprive you of space, make or mar your comfort when using the bathroom, and improve the room's visual appeal.

1 Planning

The first thing to ascertain when planning a new bathroom, i.e. one in a new house, one converted from an existing room, or built as an extension on to a house, is that it conforms with the building regulations. If you are simply doing up a bathroom, replacing old equipment and so on, this probably will not be necessary, but in any of the first three cases, it certainly will. If the room is being added as an extension, you will need planning permission from your local authority too, unless it is less than 1750 cub. ft or $\frac{1}{10}$ of the existing cubic area of the house.

If you are contemplating any major addition or alterations to a house, it is sensible to consult an architect. But if your budget is tight and you are simply converting or adding a bathroom, you can probably manage without his full services. That is, you can ask him to prepare you a scheme and submit drawings for building regulations and/or planning approval, but arrange to approach builders for prices and actually supervise the work yourself. The Royal Institute of British Architects' scale of charges for conversion work starts at about $12\frac{1}{2}$ per cent, but under the above arrangement, whereby the architect does not obtain prices or supervise the work, he would probably only charge about $\frac{2}{3}$ of the total fee. For this you would get the full benefit of his design training and aesthetic flair, plus his knowledge of building and planning regulations. It is wiser to approach a small firm of architects for this type of work, or even a single man working on his own, because a large firm will not usually take on a small job and if they do it is likely to be handled by junior staff. Whereas a youngish architect setting up on his own, perhaps with several years' experience in someone else's office, would be keen to get the work and give it his full attention. If you do not know of such an architect you can keep an eye open for schemes you admire in the home-type magazines (the architect's name is invariably given), or approach the Royal Institute of British Architects who will suggest some names.

Your finances may not even run to this limited service, or you may feel that the job is not large enough to warrant it—or that you can cope quite well on your own. In this case, be quite sure you know about the relevant building regulations. The principal ones affecting bathrooms are as follows: you may not have a bathroom and lavatory directly off a living room or kitchen or scullery—there must be a ventilated lobby in between. You may, of course, have a bathroom/lavatory directly off a bedroom. A window in a bathroom/lavatory must be 2′ square, a skylight must be $\frac{1}{5}$ of the floor area; or (and this applies to an internal room where there is no window), there must be a mechanical means of ventilation, such as a fan discharging to the outside air. But it is possible that there will be regional variations to these regulations and you should at the outset seek advice at your local authority offices. In London, the District Surveyor is the person to approach, and out of London, the Building Inspector; they will give you detailed advice concerning the Building Regulations. But if you need planning approval too, consult your local Town Planning officer.

Assuming that you intend to manage without the services of an architect or interior designer and plan your own bathroom, remember that the nearer the sanitary fittings are to the existing plumbing, the simpler and cheaper the new installation is likely to be. It is perfectly possible to take a hot water supply from one side of a house to another by means of a loop, and the same applies to drainage if there is a good fall,

1 Smooth modern bathroom in which all pipes are concealed, designed by architects Holscher and Tye who also designed the washbasin, bidet and lavatory.

but it will inevitably cost more than if all the plumbing is neatly packed into one area: if, for instance, the bathroom is above the kitchen or next door to an existing one. Similarly, when you come to plan the layout of the room itself, if the bath, lavatory and washbasin or any other equipment are neatly arranged along one wall with near access to the same pipes, they will be cheaper to install than if they are spread over a large area. But if you have a large room, plenty of money or feel that certain aesthetic consider-ations override all others anyway, it is usually possible to have the sanitary equipment where-ever you want it.

The average sizes of sanitary equipment are as follows:

Bath	5′ 6″ long overall
	2′ 4″ width overall
	1′ 11″ high
Washbasin	25″ x 18″
Lavatory	2′ 6″ projection from the wall
	16″ bowl height

Since these are only average sizes they are subject to quite amazing variations. But bear them in mind when deciding what you will put in your bathroom, whether it will contain a bidet, whether it will have a separate shower or whether there is only room for one over the bath, etc. Thus you will have a rough idea of available space. When you come to work out your arrangements in detail you must have more precise sizes, so pick the various pieces of sanitary ware you want and get their exact measurements from the manufacturers' catalogues. Don't despair if the particular model you want is too large to fit into your scheme; with the great variety on the market, you will almost certainly find a smaller one to meet your requirements.

If space is available, this is the time to consider the possibility of concealing the plumbing (certainly all the pipes, and possibly the flushing cistern too) behind a suitably clad stud-partition wall. This can be done in as small a space as 6″, and if you can spare that amount from either the length or the breadth of the room it will give a very neat, streamlined appearance, particularly in a small bathroom.

The catalogue of one sanitary ware manufacturer includes coloured shapes, in scale, of all its models, plus a piece of squared paper. You measure off the shape of your own bathroom on this paper, cut out the silhouettes of baths, lavatories and bowls and edge them around within the bathroom area until you have worked out the best arrangement. This seems a good idea for the amateur, and one that could be copied even if you do not intend to use that manufacturer's equipment. Remember to allow additional space for movement though. It is no use squeezing in a bath, a bidet, a lavatory and a shower, only to find there is inadequate space for some members of the family to use them! The following space requirements are worth remembering:

1 There should be 2′ 4″ of width alongside a bath for a man to dry himself comfortably.

2 A man standing at a washbasin should have unobstructed elbowroom of 2′ 9″, preferably 3′ 6″, i.e. 1′ 9″ out either side from the centre of the basin.

3 He should have unobstructed standing space backwards from the edge of the basin of 2′ 3″.

Of course, the order in which goods are placed along a wall will make a difference to the amount of available space. For example, if you have a bath, a washbasin and a lavatory in that order, the elbowroom needed at the washbasin can invade the airspace over the bath and the lavatory, whereas if the washbasin is in the corner of the room, the elbow space (slightly asymmetrical) will need to extend farther on the side away from the wall. Small details such as these are worth considering from the outset.

Avoid putting a bath horizontally under a window, if possible: it is extremely inconvenient to have to stand in the bath to open, shut or clean the window.

When you are planning a bathroom remember to allow wall space for a towel rail, heated or otherwise, a lavatory roll holder and cupboards.

Family habits will determine whether you want lavish or limited cupboard space in the bathroom. Some women like to make up there, in which case there should be provision for cosmetics; some like to store towels there, in which case a deep cupboard is required. In any event, it is sensible to have at least a cupboard for storing bathroom cleaning equipment, spare supplies of lavatory paper, toothpaste and soap. And if you don't want all your

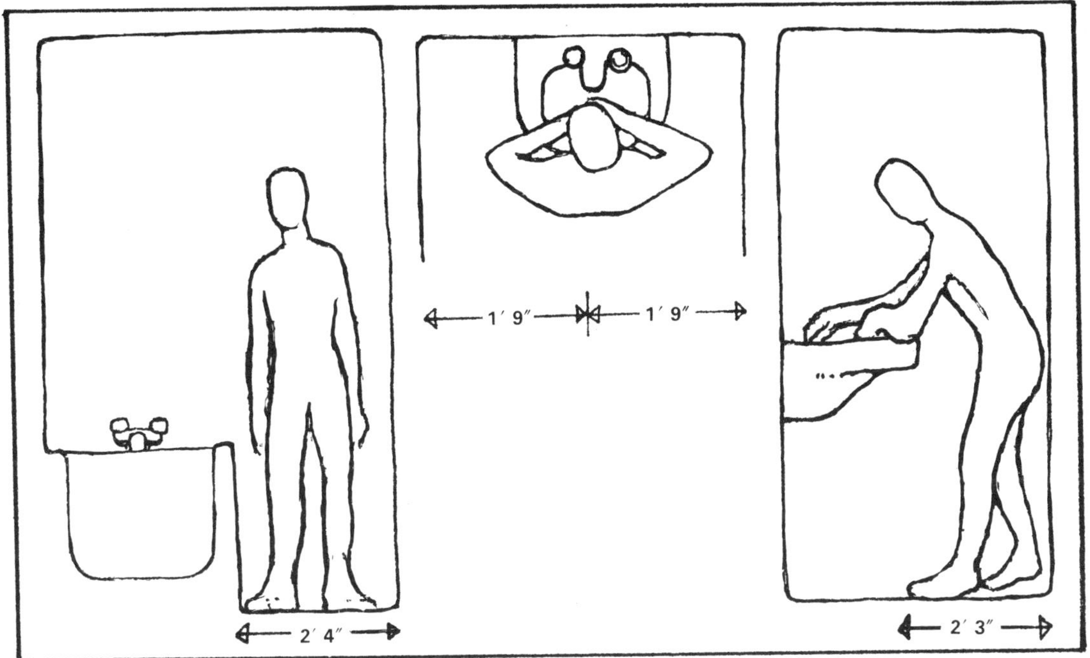

2 Useful minimum dimensions to bear in mind when planning a bathroom.

goodies on display—the main disadvantage being that they collect dust, fluff and condensation—then you will need somewhere to keep powder, bath salts, deodorants and bath oils, however decorative their containers.

A cupboard can often take the form of a vanitory unit with a washbasin set into it; or you can have a fairly shallow eye-level cupboard with sliding doors. This takes up no precious floor space and can run across the room from one wall to another above, say, the washbasin and lavatory. Or, if you have built a stud-partition to conceal your plumbing, it is possible to slip in a flush-front cupboard within that space, possibly with mirror-fronted sliding doors.

Take time over planning. Consider your requirements very carefully and those of everybody who will use the bathroom. Remember things that have irritated you in other bathrooms in the past and try not to make mistakes which it will be expensive to rectify.

It is not possible to write in an entirely general way about bathrooms because, although they are all used for the same basic human functions and activities, there are too many different types of people living in too many different sorts of accommodation, having various permutations of family and vastly different sizes of pocket, for them all to have similar bathrooms. A bathroom can be a mere slip of a room, strictly functional, or it can be a large, luxurious room, lavishly equipped and decorated; or it can be a number of things in between, such as a laundry/bathroom, an old person's bathroom, a dressing room/bathroom and so on. In the next section there will be information aimed specifically at helping the owners—or planners—of seven distinctly different types.

Mini-bathrooms

This is probably the commonest type of all, because most architects and builders, perfectly reasonably, arrange a house plan so that the largest amount of space is devoted to the living area, with the result that the bedrooms and bathrooms tend to get a bit pared down. Anyone living in a speculatively built semi-D or terrace house, whether old or new, or a detached but inexpensive modern house or modern flat, is likely to have a mini-bathroom.

But although it is small there is no reason why it should not be attractive and comfortable. To begin with it is obviously an advantage to choose the smallest items of sanitary equipment you can find, which are comfortable in use. The smallest proper bath in which you can stretch out measures 5′ long and 2′ wide by 1′ 3″ high. (There are also stepped baths and shower-trays-cum-baths which take up less space, but I shall discuss those in another section.) However, a tall, well-built man would almost certainly find it uncomfortable, in which case it would·be better to try to fit in one 5′ 6″ or even 6′ long (this is the overall length measurement). A standard sized washbasin is 25″ x 18″, and although one can get mini-basins as small as 12″ x 14″, they are really only suitable for cloakroom use. But a basin 20″ x 16″ would be perfectly adequate for family bathroom use and these are available.

If you are rearranging an old bathroom in which a lavatory had not been installed (this being in a separate cubicle room alongside, or elsewhere in the house), it would be well worthwhile trying to incorporate an extra wc at this stage. Similarly, if you are planning a new bathroom, try to include a lavatory, providing of course that there is another in the house; if not, it is probably more convenient to keep it separate With careful planning, and using some of the small sanitary ware I have already described, it is possible to get a bath, lavatory and washbasin into a room as small as 5′ x 6′.

Many types of high-level, low-level and close-coupled syphonic cisterns need up to 2′ 8″ projection from the wall, but with the specially trimmed down lines of the cistern and lavatory manufactured by one firm, this measurement is reduced to 2′ 3″ and with another, by short projection, to 2′ 0½″.

Wall-hung equipment which leaves the floor clear gives an impression of space in a cramped room. When you have fitted all your mini-equipment in, with adequate rather than surplus space around it, there are various ways in which you can make the room look larger than it is. A mirror, strategically placed to double the apparent width of the room is an old idea, but nevertheless effective.

Keeping the walls bare of clutter increases the look of space: this means no glass shelves dotted about, no ungainly towel rails, rows of jars and boxes on top of the cistern or littering the bath surround; everything must be stored away in a minimal, space-saving cupboard.

And, of course, horizontal lines used decoratively can help, such as horizontal pine-boarding on the walls, long tiles set horizontally, horizontal lipping on cupboards and so on.

If you have decided to set your washbasin in a vanitory unit (and there are many specially designed for this particular use), you will achieve not only work space on top—a good idea if a woman intends to use the bathroom for making up—but also plenty of storage beneath. This might work very well in the type of inexpensive speculative house, where there is little built-in storage, and a deep cupboard in the bathroom could be used for dirty linen, etc.

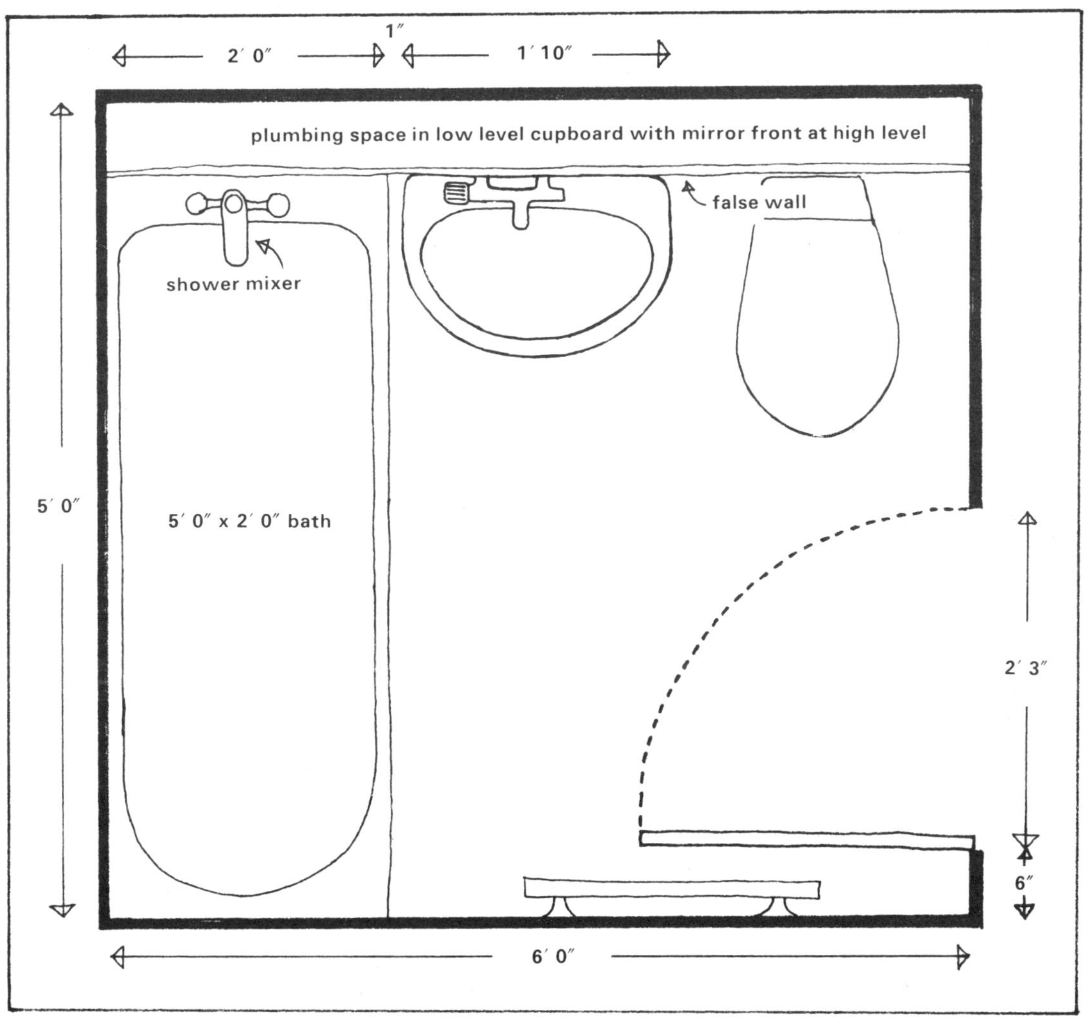

3 How to plan a bathroom with concealed plumbing
in an area 6' x 5'.

Large family bathrooms

At the opposite end of the scale from the mini-bathroom, is the large family bathroom where space is freely available and the main problem is keeping it warm. The majority of us are not blessed with this type of room, but it occurs quite often in flats in large old houses, where the convertor has clumsily allotted more than adequate space to the bathroom. Big families in older houses may also revel in the luxury of space. It is important not to squander this space though: remember that a huge bathroom can well be used for other activities.

A kitchen is a slightly suspect place in which to cope with laundry: dirty clothes, bottles of bleach and smelly steam do not really go well with hygienic food preparation. A utility or laundry room is the ideal alternative, but if this is not possible, then it is quite a good idea to fit a washing machine (particularly the automatic kind) into a large bathroom where there will also probably be room for a dirty linen box, cupboards for soap powders, etc., and possibly even an additional basin or sink for hand washing. In this case the best arrangement would be to group the bathing facilities in one part of the room and the clothes washing facilities in another, perhaps with a screen between the two. Fig 4 shows this type of arrangement for a large room. The washing machine is on an outside wall for adequate steam extraction. Obviously it is even more essential when using a bathroom for this sort of purpose that there should be at least one other separate lavatory in the house.

Although this arrangement would suit many, there are some families to whom it would be anathema; for them the bathroom means only a bath, basin, bidet, lavatory and shower, all of which can be easily fitted into the sort of large room we are discussing. Incidentally, in the event of any reader still being in ignorance about the purpose of a bidet, it is for washing your bottom. It would certainly have a place in a large family bathroom, as would a 6′ bath, able to accommodate the largest member of the household, and a capacious washbasin with a wide rim which gives a splendidly unskimped look to the room and provides a lot of splash protection when it is being used by children.

When planning a large room, do not scatter the equipment about in a reckless wastage of space. Besides making the plumbing unnecessarily expensive, this will give a disagreeably uncoordinated look to the room. If you decide to have a shower unit quite independently of the bath—a good idea when there are several children, since one can shower while another baths—they can be grouped back to back, sharing the same water supply and drainage (as in the bathroom in fig 5). For hygiene reasons, the lavatory and bidet should, ideally, be near the washbasin. Once you begin to think in this way, you have self-imposed restrictions which should lead to a sensible and logical arrangement of the equipment.

Even if your large bathroom does not double as a family laundry, it will probably be used by a variety of age groups, ranging from those who need nappies, through those who play with boats in the bath to those who have a vast array of bath cosmetics to accommodate. Unless you are to live in a perpetual chaos of possessions, this is just the bathroom for quite a large area of cupboard space. Build it in and allocate one section to each member of the family. Fig 6 shows the cupboard in architect Jacob Blacker's bathroom. This is not a large room but it is beautifully planned. The cupboard is ideal for family use, with pull-out wire trays for

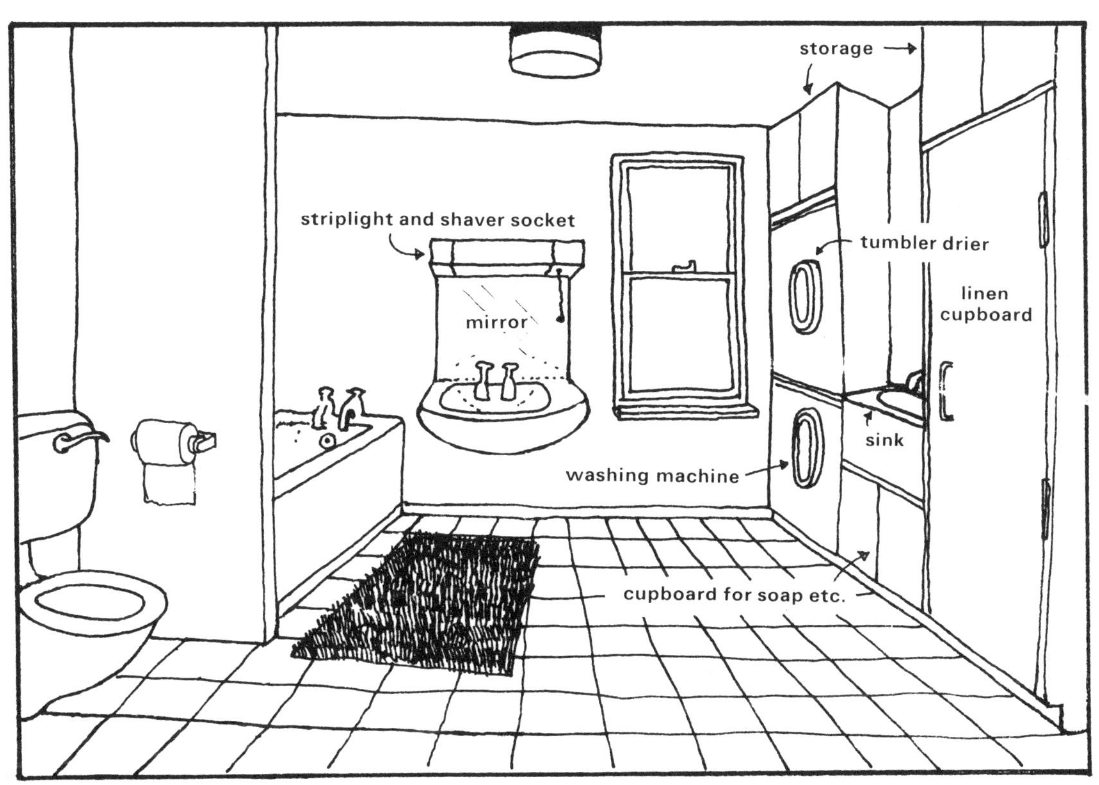

4 A large laundry-bathroom.

nappies and baby clothes at one end, storage for toys in the middle and bathroom requisites at the other end. It is also, with its set-in washbasin, a good place to bath and dress a young baby.

Another good arrangement for this purpose is suggested in fig 9. Many baby baths are designed to fit on to an ordinary bath; if the baby can then be lifted directly on to an extension of the bath itself for drying and dressing, with a cupboard underneath to store his belongings, the whole exhausting business can be carried out quite painlessly! If you are planning a big bathroom, and babies are expected, this is an idea to bear in mind.

8 A lock which can be opened from the outside should be fitted to bathroom doors used by children and old people.

non-slip floor as well as a rubber safety mat and, for maximum comfort and safety, the cubicle should be 2′ 6″ deep and 2′ 9″ wide, with a verticle grip rail on the wall opposite the seat, extending 3′ to 5′ above floor level. The shower should, whether in a cubicle or fitted above the bath, be thermostatically controlled. Sharply projecting glass shelves above washbasins should be avoided, but there should be adequate space for putting things around the basin, possibly in the form of a vanitory unit which will have low-level storage.

Special care should be taken to have a non-slip floor in bathrooms for the elderly, and if carpet is disliked for reasons of hygiene, unpolished vinyl or cork will probably be most satisfactory.

It has only been possible to give the most general outline of ideas on this specialized subject, but it can be studied in more detail in Selwyn Goldsmith's manual *Designing for the Disabled,* published by the RIBA, from which a great deal of this information was obtained.

When you have arranged for your elderly people to be comfortable and safe, give a little thought to the state of their morale. The grip rails will tend to give the bathroom a clinical appearance which can be alleviated to a great extent by cheerful decoration. Brightly coloured towels, curtains and bath mats need not be expensive, but they can change the whole feeling of a bathroom and lift the spirits of someone who is depressed by constant reminders of waning physical powers.

Children's bathrooms

In a large enough house where there are several young children in the family and the prospect of there being so for, say, ten years ahead, it is worth planning one bathroom especially for them. Some of their requirements will coincide with those of the old people; for instance the door should be unlockable from outside and there should be a non-slip floor, although in the case of child users, I would not recommend a carpet. It stands a good chance, if the children are normal, of becoming soaked and soiled in a very short while. Vinyl is the best alternative, since cork, even with a plastic finish, is liable to rise under the onslaught of constant wettings. The whole area should be impervious to splashing and easily cleaned, for this bathroom is unlikely to get the delicate treatment necessary to maintain a more elaborate form of decoration. Tiled walls are ideal, but a less expensive finish would be a fabric-backed vinyl, which can be washed down and comes in many decorative patterns. Laminated plastic is another wall finish which

9 An arrangement for bathing a baby in a normal family bathroom.

is initially expensive but, like tiles, it has a long life and is easily kept clean. One of the largest manufacturers developed a new textured range for the liner *QE2,* which was then put on to the market: this has entirely overcome the slightly cold look of the smoother laminated plastic. Fig 10 shows a bathroom by Garnett, Cloughley and Blakemore which was specially designed for the makers of the textured plastic. With every surface washable, it would make a splendid background for children. But—be warned—this type of effect could only be achieved by a good designer.

In a bathroom to be used by children of several ages, the difficulty will be to reconcile their various washing requirements. A bath with a low side (such as that used by old

10 Textured laminated plastic wall surfaces, smooth plastic vanitory unit, plastic taps and concealed lighting contribute to an immaculately detailed bathroom designed by architects Garnett, Cloughley and Blakemore.

people) is ideal for children who can bath themselves: it is not so good for a mother who has to bend double to bath younger children. A good idea is to have a bath of normal height, which will be perfectly accessible to older children, as well as making it easier for the mother to bath the very smallest, while encouraging the toddlers to use a separate shower cabinet. Again, as with old people, it is essential that both bath and shower outlets should be thermostatically controlled.

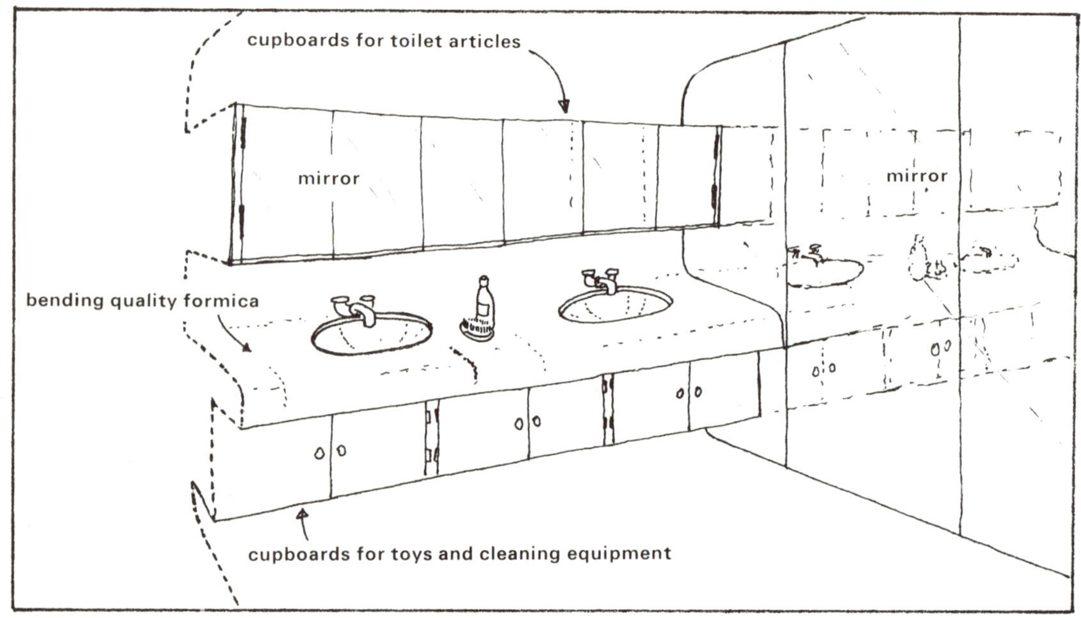

Cupboards are essential in a nursery or children's bathroom, and the sort of wall-to-wall vanitory unit shown in fig 11 is ideal; a large inset washbasin can be used for bathing the baby comfortably, if the tap is set in the wall above the basin, but there should also be another washbasin, possibly smaller, where older children can wash at the same time.

Do not have a medicine chest in a children's bathroom, unless it can be kept locked. Have light cords hung low for small hands to find easily in the middle of the night, and be extra sure that heating appliances are well out of reach.

If the children are close in age and you are prepared for a recurring expense over the years,

11 Family bathroom with two basins set into vanitory unit incorporating lots of storage space.

it is possible to start off with a 12″ high lavatory, changing this first to a 14″ then to a 16″ as they grow. They will certainly be more comfortable, independent and less likely to fall if you can afford this refinement. It is good too to have a partition wall separating the lavatory from the rest of the bathroom. Even small children who are bathed, washed and tidied *en masse* often appreciate at least semi-privacy when they are using the lavatory.

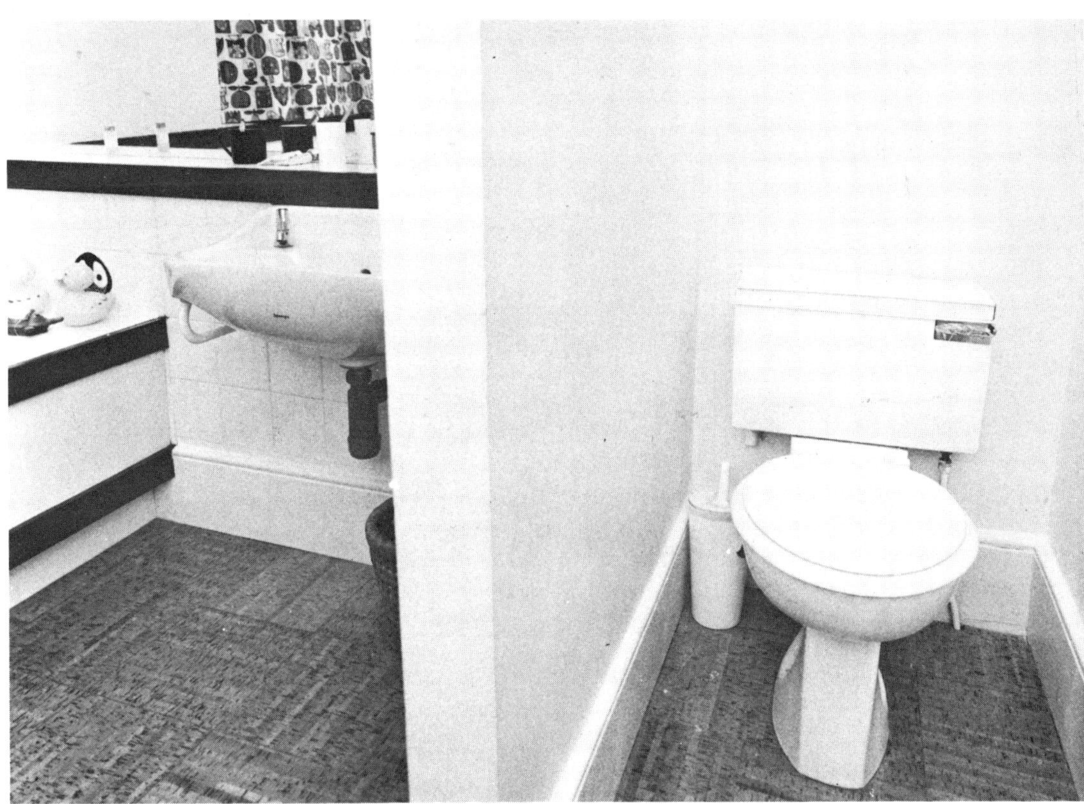

12 This children's bathroom with a warm cork floor has a 'privacy partition' between the lavatory and the rest of the room.

Shower rooms

Resistance to showers usually comes from women who prefer a relaxing soak in hot water; it is men who plump for the invigorating effects of a shower. They may be influenced by the fact that in a shower you use only a quarter of the hot water that you would in an average bath. Perhaps female resistance will be broken down with knowledge of this fact and also by the increased comfort and control which is now possible. It is no longer necessary to be deluged from above or scalded unexpectedly, when someone turns on a cold tap elsewhere in the house, or find the water reduced to a limp trickle.

Where there is only one bathroom in a house, it is often possible to fit in a small shower room which would make an enormous difference to family comfort, especially during the morning rush hour. The minimum area needed for a shower tray is 2′ 6″ square. This space could be carved out of a downstairs cloakroom which already has a washbasin and lavatory (and all the necessary plumbing), or a food storage cupboard near the kitchen which has become obsolete with the arrival of a large refrigerator, or the end of a corridor. You could even use one section of a large bedroom, in

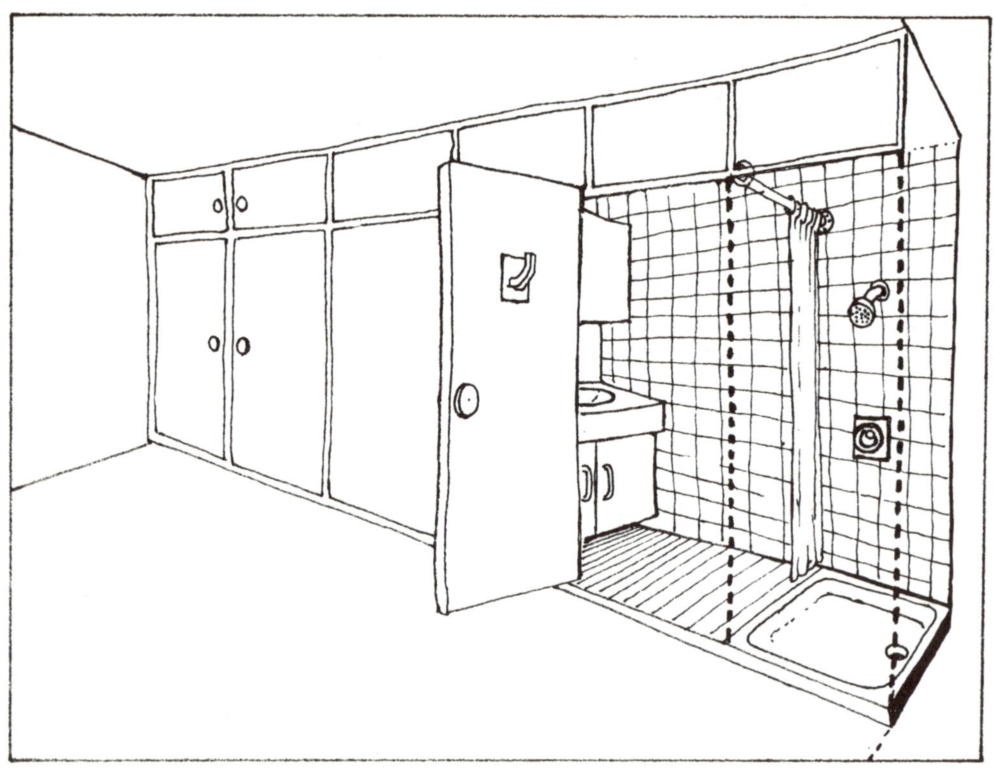

which case the shower unit could be incorporated into a complete wardrobe and dressing unit.
When you are deciding where to put a shower
room, bear the following points in mind:
1 The nearer you can get it to an existing water
   supply and drainage, the better. An ideal
   situation would be next door to an existing
   bathroom, or (as mentioned above) in an
   existing cloakroom; but this is not essential,
   it just makes the work cheaper and easier.

13 A large bedroom could contain this type of
dressing/shower unit along one wall.

2 The amount of pressure you get from the shower is governed by the distance between the bottom of the cold water system and the shower rose. The greater the distance, the more 'head' of pressure you get, and it should be at least 3′. This does not apply to the hot water supply which is fed from the cold water tank. If the head is less than 3′, which may be the case in a house with a flat roof or in a flat, first investigate the possibility of raising the tank. If this cannot be done, a pump can be installed to boost pressure. This can either be fitted on the outlet of the shower with a pressure switch, or it can be concealed nearby; but it must always be easily accessible for maintenance.

3 If you have no piped hot water supply but use an instantaneous gas or electric storage heater, it is still possible to run a shower from this, provided you choose the right type. There are several which are recommended as efficient in these circumstances (i.e. they are able to keep up a constant pressure of water), and shower manufacturers usually have a list available.

The shower cubicle itself can be bought complete if you wish. There are many on the market, some made of steel finished in vitreous enamel, some in reinforced fibreglass, some in moulded polystyrene. There is a particularly good looking one, imported from Sweden, which is supplied in knock-down form and consists of an enamelled steel tray, an aluminium hose and wired glass walls. It is easy to assemble and relatively inexpensive. All these ready-made cubicles come complete with fittings, including shower, controls, etc.—though these may be altered to meet your particular requirements—and only need to be plumbed into the water supply before they are ready for use. Your choice depends on aesthetic preferences and the price you can afford. But you may prefer to design (or have designed) your own room. You can start with a bought shower tray in cast iron, plastic or ceramic or, alternatively, make and tile your own. In either case, it is best situated in an angle where two walls meet, so that only one side need be screened, using the fourth as the shower entrance. The screening can be done with a plastic curtain hung from a curved rail, but better alternatives are a rigid screen (and there are plenty on the market in either plastic or glass) or a specially built side wall lined with a water resistant material, like ceramic tiles, mosaic, sheets of laminated plastic or vinyl coated fabric—cost being the only deciding factor.

Shower fittings are now as streamlined and efficient as most other bathroom fittings. The old days of fiddling with a pair of taps while you alternately shivered and scalded until you got exactly the right temperature are over. Now there are neatly designed fittings which combine independent control of both pressure and temperature. You can control the temperature from cold to very hot, and the spray pressure from a dribble to full force, quite separately, although the controls are on the same fitting. Even more refined, and of course more expensive, is a variation of this fitting in which the temperature is thermostatically controlled. This means an automatic temperature control to cope with an unexpected fluctuation of water from the main supply, i.e. when an adjoining wc is flushed. This is essential in a shower room used by small children or elderly people and a pleasant luxury anywhere.

The shower rose can either be fixed permanently to the wall or on the end of a flexible hose, which can be fitted into two varying

15a Acrylic shower cubicle on metal base which is on the market in France, designed by Lionel Morgaine.

b Enamelled steel tray, wired glass walls and aluminium frame combine to form this neat, easily-assembled shower cabinet imported from Norway.

14 Mosaic-lined shower-cum-bath in a house at Obernai in France designed by architects B. Hudsen and R. Heller.

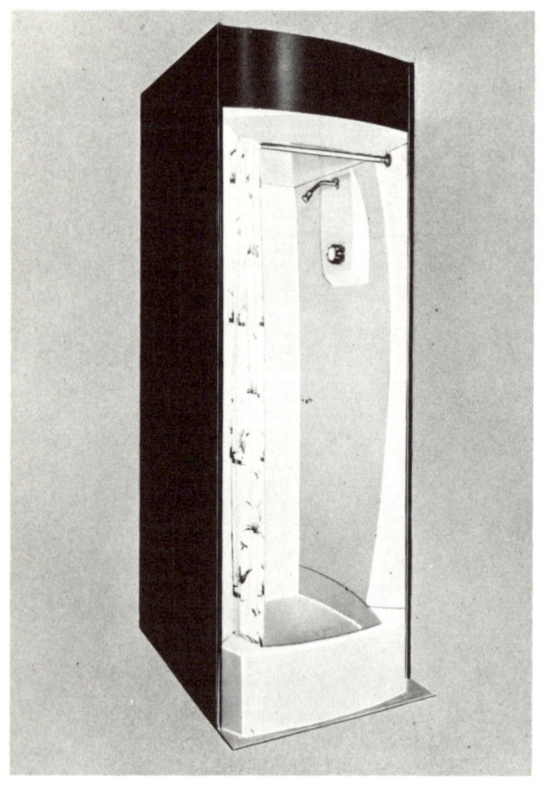

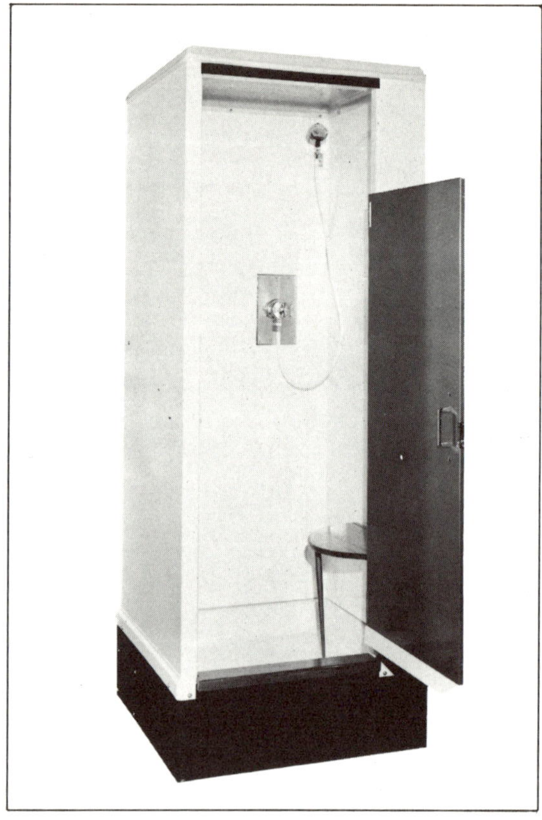

16a This glass fibre cubicle, with or without a top, comes in a specially-designed narrow size for small rooms. It can be dismantled for moving.

b Enamelled steel shower cubicle with seat and step in teak.

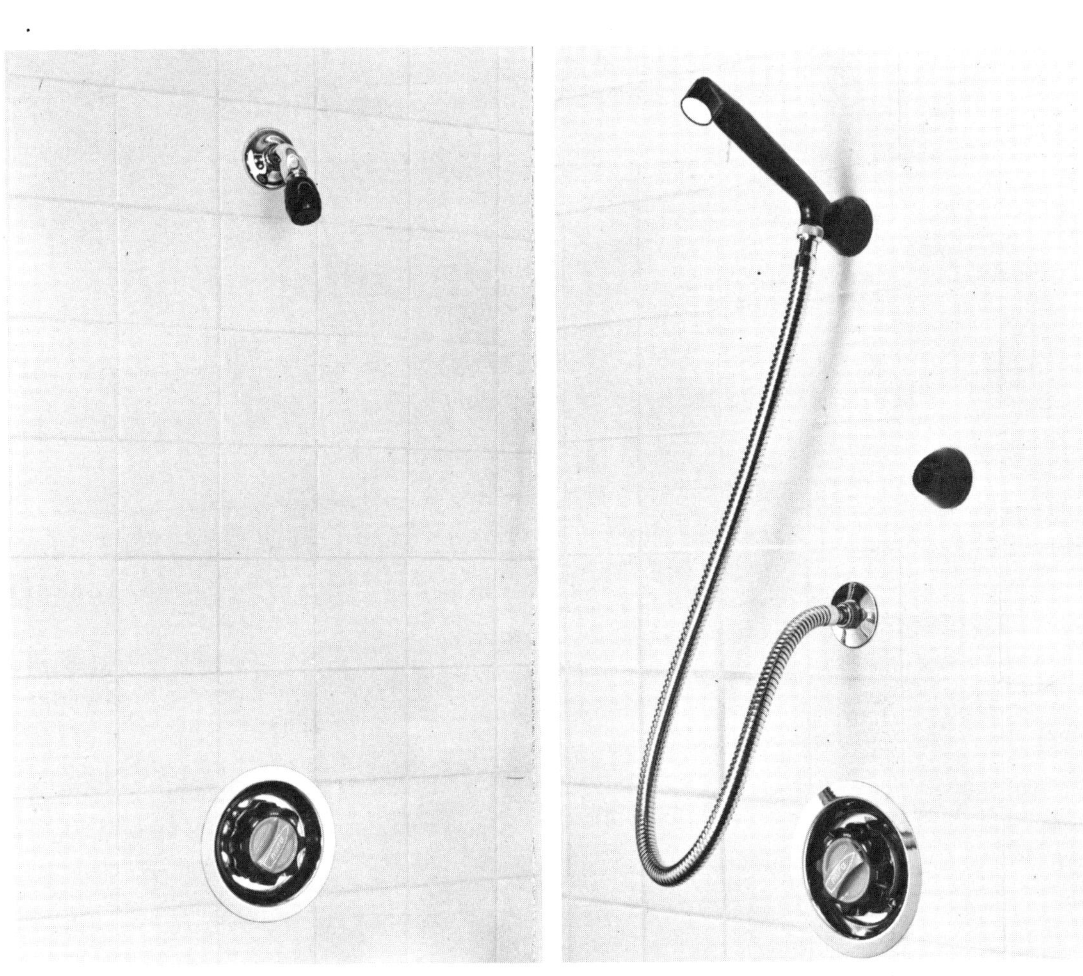

17a, b Neat shower mixing tap which allows independent selection of spray force and temperature.

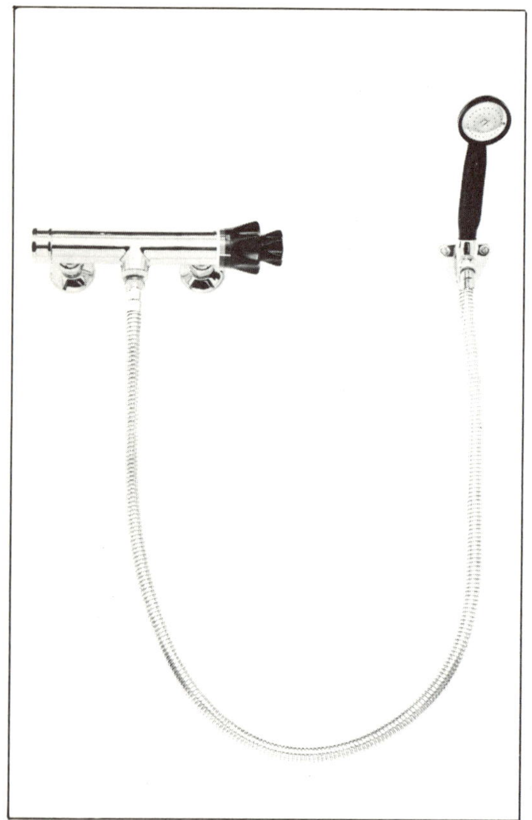

19 Made in enamelled cast iron or Perspex, this mini-bath, 36″ x 36″ x 18″, could also be used as a shower tray.

◀ **18** Thermostatic mixer used with a flexible tube and handspray assembly.

height sockets on the wall, usually at shoulder height or above head height. In either case, a much neater appearance is achieved if the pipes are concealed.

Although the minimum sized shower is only 30″ x 30″, they can be considerably larger, especially if you choose to build your own. The one in fig 19 measures only 3′ x 3′ and

is 18″ deep; and in addition to being a shower tray it can be used as a small, two-level bath. A typical British compromise, this would raise your shower room to the level of a mini-bathroom, and would be particularly suitable for young children. There are similar dual-purpose units available, but none smaller than this.

20a, b German version of 'pod' bathroom by Hans Gunter Möller available in several pastel colours.

Prefabricated bathrooms

Industrialized building, despite many written words extolling its virtues and benefits, is still in the throes of a frail infancy. Most people prefer to invest their precious cash in bricks and mortar rather than in an unfamiliar, factory-made product which they cannot accept as a real house. And this prejudice is reflected in the building societies' attitude to lending on an unconventional structure. There is a slightly less reactionary attitude to components, perhaps because they involve less expenditure. Many people quite happily tack on a factory-made room to extend their home, or house their car in a prefabricated garage, or install a 'heart unit' which will provide plumbing and hot water for all the business parts of the house. It is now possible to buy bathrooms off-the-peg, some complete down to the family toothbrush holder, and attach them to an existing home. This is a quick, uncomplicated way of acquiring a bathroom if you have neither the time nor the interest to cope with the building of a custom-made job.

One firm has been selling complete, prefabricated bathrooms for some years now. Traditional in design and content, they are contained in a timber stud and blockboard box which can be lifted into place by crane, attached to the outside of a house and then rendered to merge in with the existing building. The whole process is quick, clean and inexpensive when done on a large scale, and the resulting

interior is quite indistinguishable from that of a normal brickbuilt bathroom. Until now these package bathrooms have only been widely used in the rehabilitation or building programmes of local authority estates, or in large scale installations for hostels, motels, etc., but the idea is perfectly feasible, both financially and practically, for one-off jobs; and the manufacturers are currently working on plans for this sort of installation.

More exciting to look at, and with an eventual greater development potential, are the glass fibre reinforced plastic bathrooms, which have gradually been appearing on the market in many countries during the last year or two. Again, their manufacturers hope to capture the large markets offered by local authority and private developments, but their products are also available to the private purchaser. In order to minimize stress concentration at junction points of ceiling, walls, floor and door openings, these areas are smoothly curved, thus not only fulfilling the primary objective of strengthening the structure, but also giving an attractive streamlined appearance which is particularly appropriate in a bathroom. One of the most interesting and advanced of these GRP bathrooms is based on a number of horizontal components which pack one inside the other for easy transport, and can be carried through normal sized doorways for erection within a house. Plumbing and drainage is flexibly designed to meet various local authority requirements and the room can be put up on screeded or unscreeded concrete floors, or direct on to timber joists. Fittings vary according to whether you have a de-luxe or standard model (the former including a heated towel rail, electric shaver socket, light fitting and so on), but in either case the smooth glossy gell coating gives a hygienic and easily cleaned finish. The standard colour is pale blue; other colours can be specially ordered. Prices for this 'pod' bathroom, whose makers promise a long, maintenance-free life, are extremely reasonable, and since they include delivery and positioning on site the only extras would be for labour involved in fixing them to existing services.

Prefabricated bathrooms are not widely used, nor are there an enormous number on the market—as yet. But they have been tested in use. A specially designed version was installed in the Habitat block of flats at Montreal for Expo 67: it is available in this country—and for a householder not hidebound by convention and with a taste for simplicity, they are definitely worth investigating.

21 *Opposite:* Glass fibre 'pod' bathroom assembled from horizontal components which allow for easy packing and transport.

Luxury bathrooms

A small, inexpensive bathroom can be so planned and fitted that it is the epitomy of comfort. But real luxury is more than this. It only exists when cost is of little importance, space is ample and the whole atmosphere is one of sybaritic abandon, rather than tight-lipped good sense.

First in the United States and then, inevitably, in Europe, manufacturers have been fostering the idea of the bathroom as a place for relaxation and pleasure rather than for a top-speed cleansing operation. In fact one manufacturer suggests we should all have a shower room for washing and a beautifully decorated and furnished bathroom for soaking and relaxing—which is what the Japanese have been doing for centuries. Assuming your luxury bathroom is kept at a constantly warm temperature by central heating (and you are hardly likely to wallow in expensive splendour till you can at least afford some warmth), there is likely to be

22 A rosy-patterned fabric has been bonded into this armchair-shaped glass fibre bath, designed by Geoffrey Bonsack.

23 By raising the floor of this small bathroom with its folding louvred doors, architect Edward Samuel has achieved a sunken-tub effect.

little trouble with steam and condensation. So pictures can be hung, silk curtains draped at the windows, expensive carpets laid on the floor and upholstered furniture brought in, with no threat of condensation damage. Make doubly sure though by installing an extractor fan.

A large bath suggests luxury to many people —it is not only expensive to buy, but costs more to fill with hot water. Several of the most capacious can accommodate two people at a time and have their taps and outlet arranged with this eventuality in mind. Even grander is the sunken tub which, I hasten to add, is a

24 Lighting, storage and wall cladding are all beautifully detailed in this sauna bath designed by Ralph Erskine for his home in Sweden.

physical impossibility in many modern houses. You simply cannot sink some 23 ″ of bath into 8 ″ or so of joist space. Conversions offer a lot more scope, especially if high ceilings on the ground floor are being lowered, leaving several feet above which could easily contain the bottom end of a sunken bath. Or it could be arranged to protrude into the dead storage area of a built-in cupboard. The sunken bath shown in fig 23 has been cleverly achieved by raising the level of the floor, so that you step up into the room and then down into the bath.

No need to skimp on colour in this luxury bathroom, where you can presumably replace anything which bores you after a few years. Pattern can cover the bath and washbasin as well as the walls, since one shrewd manufacturer discovered how to insert layers of fabric, glittering aluminium dust or hand-painted designs into his resin-bonded glass fibre equipment. Warm to the touch (another weapon against steam), available in over 20 colours, and with baths from round to trapezium shaped, this range would undoubtedly offend the purist in his white-tiled cubicle. For the luxury-lover it opens up immense decorative possibilities, and apparently the export side of the business is booming.

There is a grand old hotel in Hamburg where the luxury suites have double bathrooms, with one bath for him and one for her. Although few households can aspire to this sort of splendour, the beautiful mosaic-lined bath tub and washbasin shown in fig 36 might make a very acceptable alternative. It was designed by architect Michael Blee for clients who like to bath *à deux*, often drinking wine and generally relaxing at the same time. To achieve the necessary firm foundation for the rich amber mosaic, the first-floor bath is built up in solid brickwork over a reinforced concrete slab, with the corners of the bath and washbasin formed by hand in cement mortar to specially prepared full-size templates. The resulting bathroom has wide shelves and a dressing table lined in mosaic, a specially-made mirror, walls covered in pine treated with matt poly-urethane lacquer and a fitted carpet. There is space for people, places to put wine bottles, glasses, candles and books, all of which figure in the true sybarite's bathing habits.

In Finland, sauna baths are installed in every house and many public buildings. We tend to class them with bidets as something odd used by foreigners, but this attitude, like many others, is slowly changing. For the present, however, sauna bathrooms come into the luxury category. Smelling deliciously of their wood lining, they can be custom built, preferably close to a bathroom or swimming pool; the idea is that after baking in a dry heat up to as much as 250°F, you plunge your body into the invigorating cold of a pool or shower. Several prefabricated and relatively inexpensive sauna units, complete with electric stoves, are imported and these could easily be erected in a spare room or in the garden close to the pool. One man I know acquired the taste on business trips to Scandinavia and only sleeps well after a session in his sauna. The custom-built sauna in fig 24 belongs to British architect, Ralph Erskine, who lives and works in Sweden; this one has been skilfully incorporated into a normal bathroom.

This seems the obvious place to mention gold-plated taps and accessories; the former may be disguised as dolphins, swans or shells, or even left to look like taps. For the more restrained, there are expensive but simple chromium-plated fittings which give an impression of unostentatious luxury—even if your bath is the one with a marble surround shown in fig 25.

25 Large luxurious bath with wide seat-surround in marble, remote control taps and waste and stand for holding bathtime snacks, drinks, etc.

Baths

Baths are made in several materials and a great variety of shapes. Still the most popular, because they are considered to be the toughest, are enamelled, pressed steel or cast iron baths. They are also the most expensive. Making small but increasing inroads into sales figures are acrylic sheet baths (which in England means ICI Perspex). These have the advantage of being light to transport, non-corroding and instantly warm to touch and they cost the same in colour as they do in white. They scratch if you dig at them with a sharp instrument (but so does enamel), although the scratch can be removed with metal polish. And of course they are easily moulded into a variety of undulating shapes; in fact the side panels provided with some models look as though they came from a jelly mould. Their major disadvantage, and one which makes them unacceptable in the hotel world, is that they burn if they come into contact with a lighted cigarette. As one manufacturer says mournfully, 'The things people will do in a hotel bathroom, that they would never do at home . . . .' But for a reasonably house-trained family who want some colour in the bathroom without too much expense they are a good alternative to an enamelled bath.

Care has to be taken too with the baths made of glass fibre reinforced resins I mentioned on

26a For a small extra charge one company will finely sand-blast the surface of any of its porcelain-enamelled baths to make it non-slip.
b Raised anti-slip surface offered by another manufacturer.

page 35, which should be considered mainly for luxury bathrooms where aesthetic may override practical considerations. These can be made in innumerable colours, with any fabric the purchaser fancies bonded into their shape. But they must only be cleaned with liquid soap, they soften slightly if filled with very hot water and, of course, they are expensive. They would not instantly spring to mind as the best buy for a bathroom which is frequently used by mud-caked children—or gardeners.

Bath shapes vary from the lean and simple to the undulating and elaborate. Whether you want the former, the latter or something in between, your taste will almost certainly have been anticipated. You may want one grab rail or two, or scorn the need for either. Baths can have a flat or a curved bottom and at least two manufacturers will provide a special anti-slip treatment. The choice is yours. Since a large firm of sanitary ware manufacturers in the United States financed an investigation into all aspects of bathroom use, their subsidiary in England has produced a Perspex bath, whose shape tries to cater for every conceivable bathing activity! Another company, working along the same lines, has produced a bath which is so relaxing it has a rubber covered foam cushion to accommodate the lolling head.

a

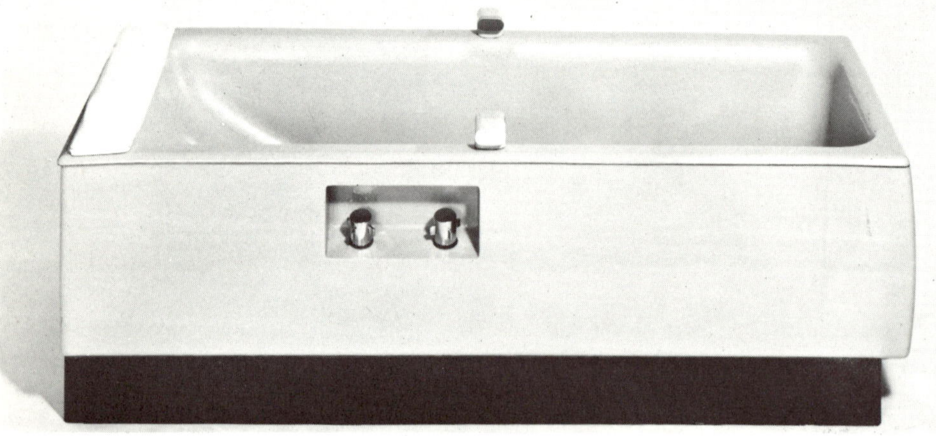

b

c

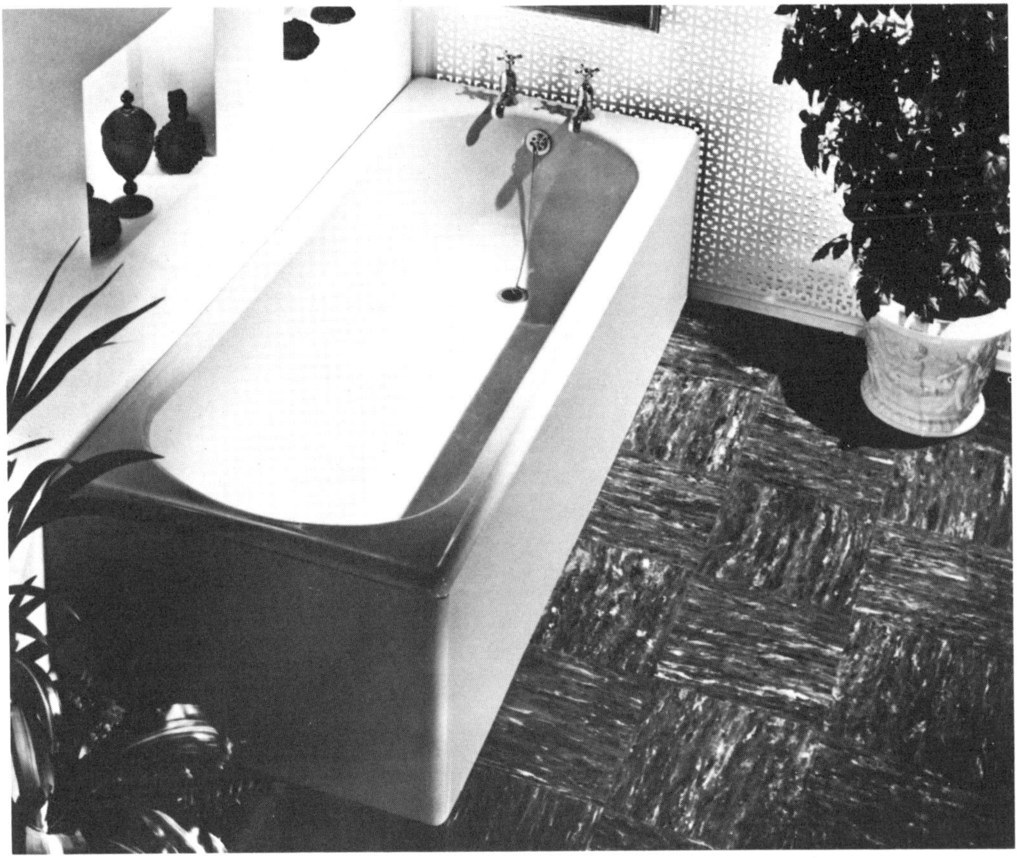

d

27a Spacious glass fibre corner bath available in
   several pastel colours.
  b Porcelain enamelled cast iron bath specially con-
   toured for comfort: it has a chainless semi-
   captive plug, a soft headrest and taps mounted
   outside.
  c Ergonomically-designed bath based on American
   research has a long soap shelf and corner-
   mounted taps.
  d Simple Perspex bath which avoids some of the
   excessive decoration often inspired by the
   moulding qualities of the material.
  e Double bath with padded headrest and quilted
   bath panels is made in glass fibre and is available
   in numerous colours.

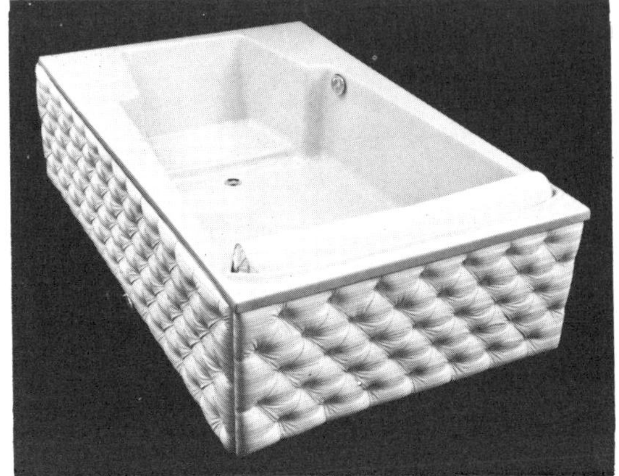

e

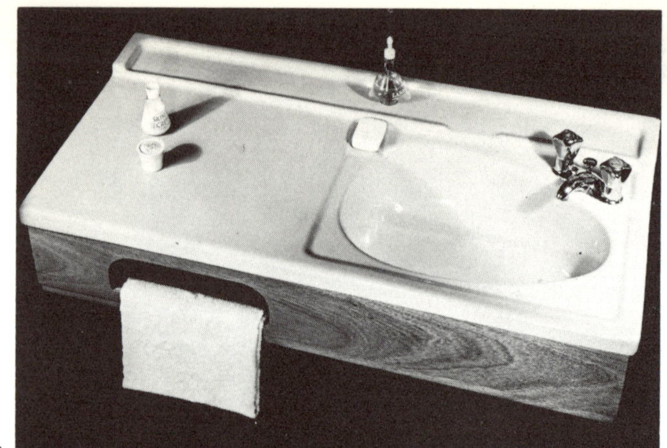

28a This vanitory top with integral towel rail would fit neatly into a small bathroom.
  b Neat corner basin available in two sizes.
  c Perspex washbasin available in several colours can be fitted into counter tops.
  d Elegant washbasin with useful wide shelf.

29 Basin 21″ x 17″ designed for fitting into a counter top with a metal frame.

The size of your bath will depend on your shape, your pocket and the area of your bathroom. Apart from the 3′ x 3′ mini-bath mentioned earlier there are old-fashioned hip-baths in which you sit rather than lie and which are often used by old people. About 3′ 7″ long, one of these could be fitted into a room too narrow to take a full-length bath. Standard baths start at 4′ 6″ in length and go up to 6′, varying in width from 2′ 2″ to 2′ 6″. But for customers with more esoteric requirements, they come both wider and longer, circular and oval.

Washbasins

These are traditionally made of vitreous china, the main disadvantage of which is that it cracks if you drop something heavy into it (not an everyday occurrence), and that it costs more in colour. Like baths, basins are now also made in acrylic sheet and fibreglass, and these have the same inherent advantages and disadvantages as do the baths. There are washbasins in sizes and shapes to suit most spaces, from the smallest, which are really only suitable for a quick hand-rinse in the cloakroom, to the most expansive which include a shelf all round. There are basins which are fitted on wall brackets, or on pedestals and there are at least two, supremely elegant and sculptural, which are not only mounted on wall brackets, but conceal all pipes within their own shape. There are lots of washbowls to fit into corners and, of course, others specially designed to set into vanitory units. One, based on the American research into bathroom requirements mentioned earlier, has attempted to accommodate hand, face and hair washing activities in a basin which is longer than usual from back to front.

The amount of shelf space contained in each basin varies enormously, some having practically none, some having one soap recess, others two and so on. But it seems sensible for anyone planning a bathroom which will be subjected to normally heavy use (with people washing themselves, their hair and their stockings and possibly wetting mascara brushes, shaving and cleaning their brushes and combs) to have not only a capacious bowl, but a fairly wide shelf too. One admires the flower-like grace of those slim-rimmed bowls which have practically none, but questions their usefulness. Wide shelves prevent a wet floor and can be used as temporary resting places for all the things which come to be used and washed in a bathroom. Basins set into vanitory units or wide, built-in shelves have the same effect.

30a Another basin with completely concealed pipes which has recently come onto the market.

b Counter top basin measuring 24″ x 20″.

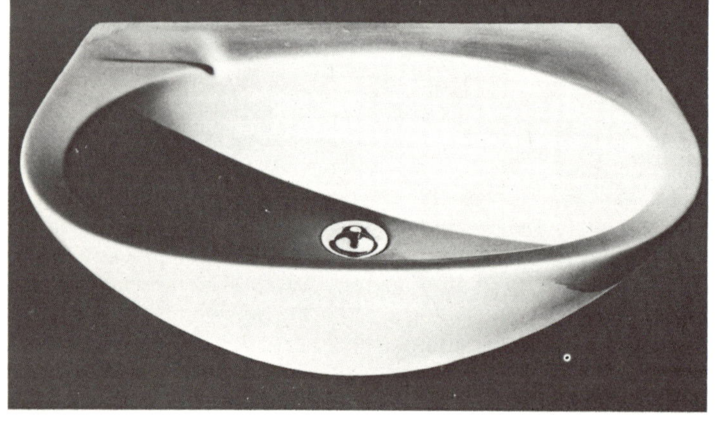

c Beautifully elegant and simple washbasin which conceals all plumbing pipes within its own shape.

31 a This washbasin, based on American research, has an anti-splash rim and is large enough for hair washing.

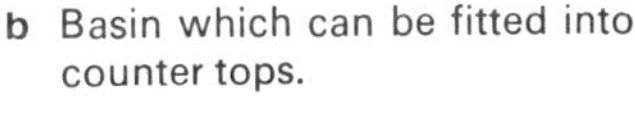

b Basin which can be fitted into counter tops.

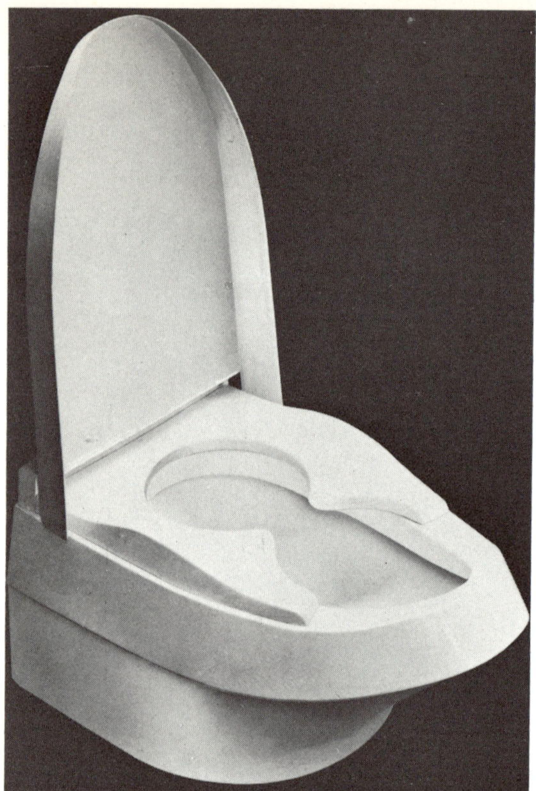

a

b

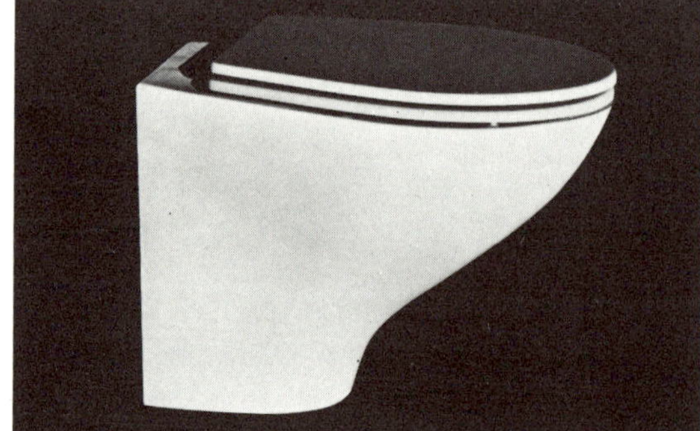

c

d

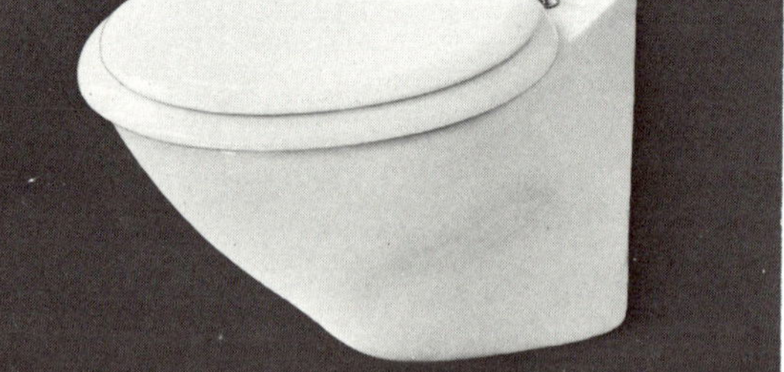

32a Prototype of lavatory designed for comfort: it is only 9″ high.

b Concealed cistern operated by remote flushing lever which could, if desired, be mounted on the floor for foot operation.

c Syphonic lavatory of unusual elegance with concealed cistern.

d This cantilevered washdown lavatory has a concealed cistern.

Opposite

e The pan of this close-coupled lavatory suite is an inch lower than the usual 16″.

33a One of the polystyrene cisterns which is now on the market.

b A plastic flush panel cistern with push-button control. It projects only 4½″ and is ideal when converting a high-level unit to low-level.

c A concealed cistern which fits into a 6″ space.

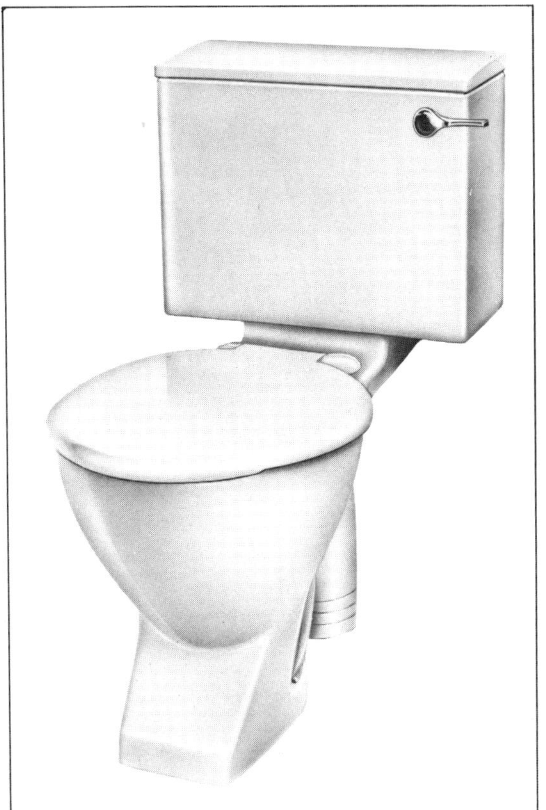

e

a

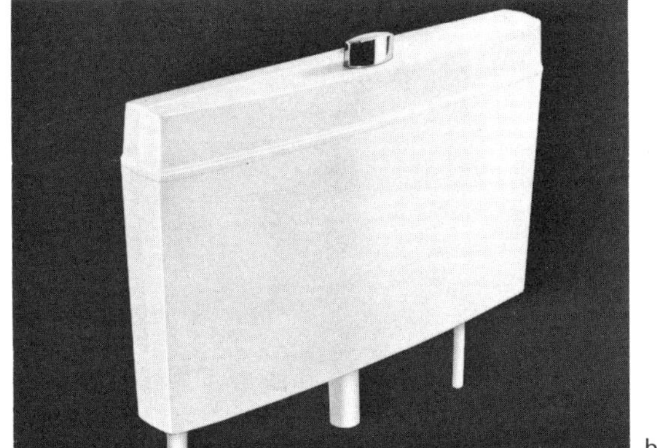

b

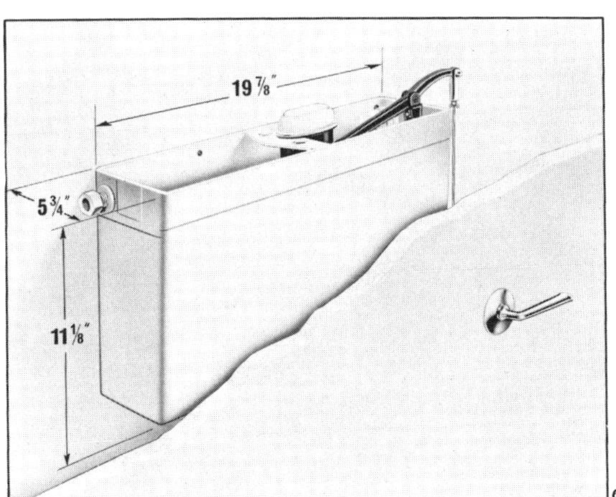

c

Lavatories

Almost the opposite applies to lavatories, which can be as slim and unobtrusive as possible and still practical. Normally only made in vitreous china, they can have either a syphonic or a wash-down flush, the former sucking the waste away, the latter pushing. Syphonic flushes are quieter, have a reputed slight tendency to blockage and are more expensive than the wash-down type. Lavatory cisterns can be mounted high or low on the wall, or they can be close-coupled to the wc pan; they are now available in thermoplastics as well as the traditional vitreous china. In the interests of mini-bathroom owners (and this, let's face it, means the majority of us) they are being streamlined to minimal dimensions. One, which is made of plastic, is panel shaped, only 4½" deep and is operated by a press button on the top. It is so designed that very often the owner of an old-fashioned high-level lavatory unit can convert it to low level with the use of this panel cistern without needing to move the existing soil pipe. In a bathroom where all plumbing is concealed within a partition wall (as described earlier) there is no reason why the lavatory cistern should not join it. There are both plastic and steel cisterns, specially designed for this purpose, which fit into a space only 6" deep, and the whole smooth operation can be completed if you wish by a chromium-plated push-lever flush control, rather than by a projecting handle or knob. This can be fitted to the floor or the wall, depending on whether you prefer to use your foot or hand for flushing.

Cantilevered lavatories, which are made by several firms, leave the floor clear for easy cleaning. They are both hygienic and space-saving and because they sit in their own concealed steel 'chair' which takes the weight they can be mounted on the lightest of partition walls.

The British Standard height for a lavatory is 16" from floor to rim. This has never been strictly adhered to by all manufacturers and the tendency now, on medical recommendation, is for lavatory pans to get lower and lower. The ultimate may have been reached in the prototype lavatory shown in fig 32a which again is a direct result of the American research and is only 9" high.

Bidets

Contrary to a popular misconception, bidets are intended to be used not only by women, but by men and children too, so they should have a place in every well-equipped bathroom if space allows. However, if, as happens in some families, inhibitions are going to prevent its everyday use, it seems pointless to spend money on one just so that it can sit there looking fashionable. Do not bother with one, or, better still, get rid of the inhibitions. They stem, apparently, from the fact that many men, both British and American, because of wartime experiences in France, associate bidets with tarts!

Many firms who make lavatory pans now make bidets too, and, like lavatories, they can either be floor-mounted or cantilevered, with concealed plumbing. There are still some which are supplied from taps mounted on the rim, so that you fill the bowl to use them. More common though are those with an ascending spray and a rim flush, and these are subject to strict Water Board and Building Regulations which, though easily conformed with in a new building, may present almost insuperable difficulties for the convertor. They must, for instance, have both hot and cold water carried from the storage supply in individual pipes, and drainage must be into a vented soil pipe rather than an open gulley. In other words, for plumbing purposes and to ensure there is no danger of back flushing which will cause a health hazard, they have to be treated as lavatories rather than washbowls. Like lavatories, they are usually made in vitreous china.

a

b

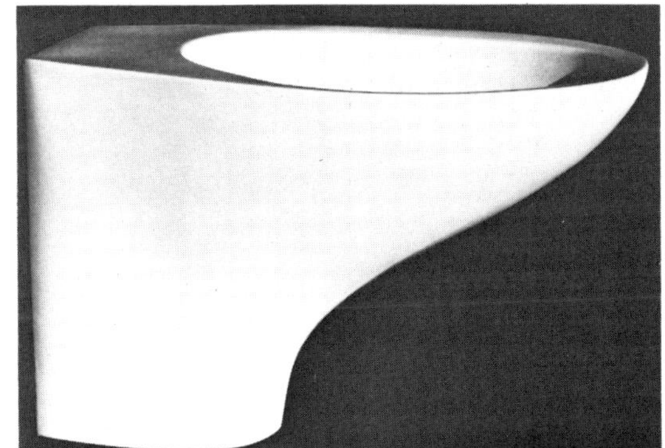

c

34a This bidet has no douche but a tap set on the rim.
  b A wall-mounted bidet which can have a douche or supply to the rim.
  c A bidet designed for wall-mounted plumbing.
  d A wall-mounted bidet with douche and rim supply.

d

Bathroom accessories

However well planned a bathroom, however satisfactory the major items of sanitary ware, it can be a constant source of irritation and discomfort if accessories like taps, soap dishes, heaters, extractors, etc., do not function as you want them to. They merit careful choice.

Tap fittings

People with the time and inclination could spend hours browsing through brochures showing the variety of tap fittings on the market, especially if they have to fit up a bath, a basin, a bidet and a shower. There are hundreds.

Some of those available for showers were described in the section on shower rooms, but since showers are also frequently fitted over baths there are controls available which serve a

35 A simple twin-dial fitting gives independent temperature and pressure control for both bath and shower.

dual purpose. With two taps for the bath, a lever for the shower, one outlet and a telephone type cradle—and sometimes a thermostatic mixing control tap—these often look distressingly complicated and are difficult to keep clean. But one firm has now produced a piece of equipment which, with a dual dial for controlling water heat and pressure for both bath and shower, is felicitously simple to operate and clean.

36 A mosaic-lined double bath and washbasin of
Roman splendour. Designed by architect Michael
Blee for a country house extension.

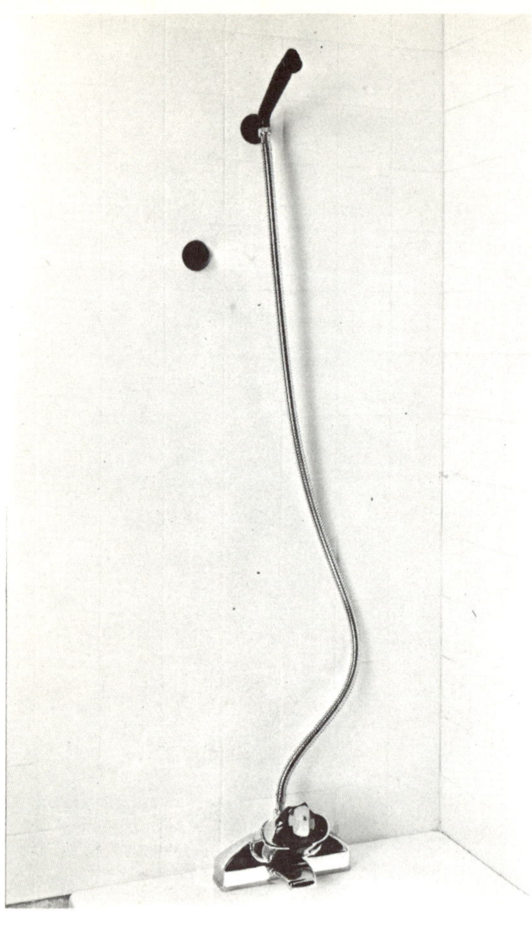

37 Twin-dial fitting from **35** shown in position.

38 a Elegant high-riding tap makes cleaning easy.
   b Wall-mounted bath taps and mixer.

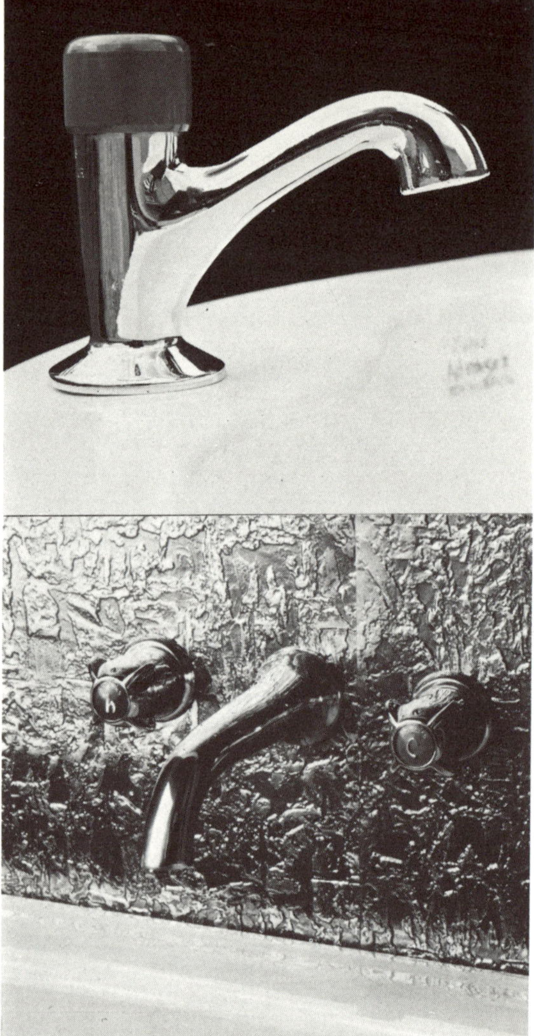

Even without a **shower fitting** on the bath, there are still a confusing number of options open to you. And the **various pieces of equipment** now become similar to those for use on washbasins, except that they are larger. In each case, you can have individual taps with a chain and plug waste outlet; or a mixer tap, with a chain and plug; or a mixer tap with a pop-up waste (plug operated by a knob or lever) fitted to the basin or to the tap. Shapes and sizes vary with each manufacturer.

Alternatively, if you have concealed plumbing, you can have any of the above arrangements mounted on to the partition wall above the bath or basin. Some of these, in addition to leaving the shelf of the bowl or bath clear, are

50

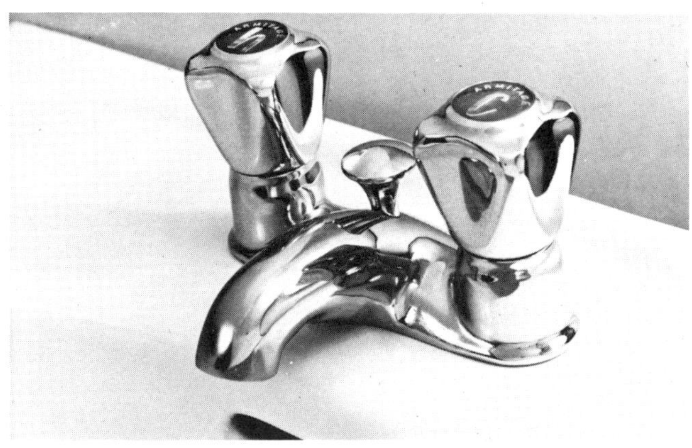

39a Taps, mixer and pop-up waste for basin combined in one fitting.

b Washbasin taps with separate mixer and chain waste.

exceptionally elegant. Smeary, ill-kept taps and fittings spoil the looks of even the most luxuriously appointed bathroom, so for those without unlimited domestic help, the simplest designs would be the best bet. It is difficult to clean around taps which crouch low against the basin or bath, and these are best avoided, along with the little patch of filth which accumulates beneath them.

Similar taps and pop-up wastes are available for bidets, but these often have special additional fittings for douche control.

There are now plastic taps on the market, and a new range with smooth, wipe-clean shapes matched by smooth, non-furring interiors, comes in white and several pastel colours. They have translucent, tinted cross-heads, they stay cool to the touch even when running very hot water and are specially designed to avoid splashing; a splendid new bathroom accessory for colour addicts.

Most sanitary ware has a predetermined position for the fitting of taps, etc., and this is no longer necessarily at the foot of the bath or the centre of the washbasin. Several baths have tap fittings at the side, where they are accessible without any effort, and don't get in the way of people sitting one at each end. Others have them diagonally across one corner, for no immediately apparent reason, and occasionally

40a Washbasin taps and mixer combined with pop-up waste.

b Plastic taps with translucent cross-heads and a 'flow-straightener' which stops splashing.

c Wall-mounted control and mixer combined. One turn gives cold water, two, hot.

the outlet is situated in a different place from the taps so that you can run in hot water while letting out cold. But normally, whatever their position, the choice of the fittings is up to the purchaser. One bath, however, that with the foam headrest described on page 37, has both taps and waste plug endemic to the design. The former are mounted in a recess on the outside panel of the bath and the latter on the rim. If you buy that particular bath, those are the unconventional fittings you get.

Mirrors

Well-placed mirrors can make a small bathroom look larger, and a large one positively palatial. But choose their positioning with care or you may find yourself confronted with unexpected and unwelcome views at defenceless moments. Probably only the young and beautiful would want to suffer a full-length mirror anywhere in a bathroom, although this is a very personal matter and not one on which I propose to pontificate. Let me simply warn you to consider all the implications of large areas of mirror before buying. Avoid having mirrors too close to washbasins, where they will get splattered with spots of soap and toothpaste which are the devil to remove, and again, if the condensation problem has not been beaten, remember that mirror-glass attracts steam like needles to a magnet, although cleaning with methylated spirit is some deterrent.

If I sound less than enthusiastic about the wholesale use of mirrors, it is not because they have any intrinsic properties which I dislike, simply that they so often conflict with bathroom requirements. In small, deliberately chosen areas, they can do much to increase apparent size, and, strategically placed behind, say, a mass of plants or a row of handsome bottles or ornaments, they will greatly boost the effect. But used in larger quantities, especially on facing walls, they are often a menace, reflecting row upon row of tooth mugs and towel rails (of all mundane objects) into infinity, proclaiming the lavatory over and over again, elongating the bath beyond any reasonable length and demanding constant and hard-rubbing attention to keep them clean. One of the most restless and discordant rooms I have ever seen was a bathroom with mirrors on two walls, a stainless steel ceiling and glossy, reflective laminated plastic on practically every other surface. The effect was distracting and unsympathetic, and should serve as a restraint to anyone gaily and thoughtlessly contemplating 'the use of mirrors' in a bathroom.

Another disadvantage which afflicts mirrors intended for bathrooms is that they are heavy and, especially when they are large, need extremely painstaking installation if they are not to be damaged. A lightweight mirror which was developed for use on aircraft and which consists of an aluminium-coated plastic film stretched over a backing of expanded polyurethane, is easily mounted into place, virtually untroubled by condensation, and therefore very satisfactory for bathroom use. It is tough, it will not shatter but it can be pierced by a sharp instrument. If you fancy a mirrored ceiling (but again be sure you consider the implications before embarking on this piece of whimsy!) this light, non-misting and relatively inexpensive product would do the job admirably.

On a less exalted plane, innumerable mirror-fronted bathroom cupboards are on the market, some fitted with electric shaver sockets and integral lights, which satisfactorily fulfil several purposes in the small bathroom.

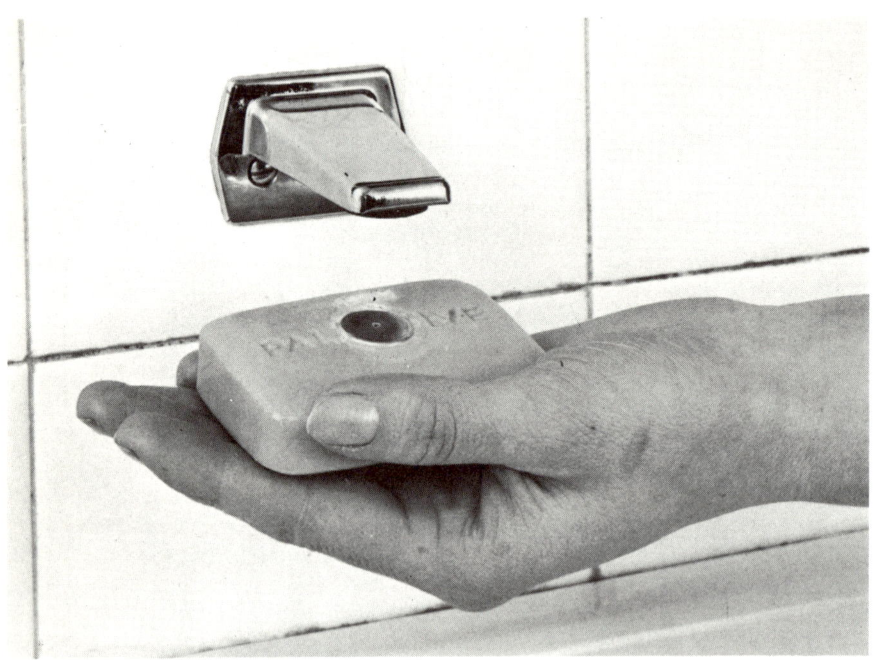

Soap dishes, etc.

If your bath or washbasin has not got a recess for soap, you will need to provide a holder on the wall above. If this is tiled, a recessed or semi-recessed holder made by a tiling manufacturer to fit exactly into their standard tile sizes (6″ x 6″ or 4½″ x 4½″) is probably the best solution. You can have a colour to match the tiles, and some makes have the beautiful sculptural quality that is appearing in washbasins, or there are chromium-plated soap dishes. Also on the market is an ingenious magnetic fixture which holds the soap from

41 Magnetic soap holder which can be mounted above bath or basin.

42 A really large wooden towel rail is mounted above the heating element in this bathroom designed by architects Roy Stout and Patrick Litchfield.

above when it is not in use. This seems an ideal solution, since it not only dispenses with those slimy messes which gather in soap dishes, whatever they are made of, but it also saves the soap.

43 Designer Peter Moll has set his washbowl in a Victorian chiffonier, inverted, painted white and mounted on the wall. There is ample storage for bathroom paraphernalia and a very decorative high-level mirror.

44 Another view of Jacob Blacker's bathroom (see fig 6) with a high-level shelf formed by the wood-lined partition which conceals plumbing and storage. A shower cubicle backs on to the bath, far right.

Holders for toothbrushes and mugs also come in china or stainless steel, but if there is a cupboard close to the washbowl—and there should be—the whole lot is better stowed away there. They gather no dust and there is one less piece of equipment to wipe free of soap splashes.

Lavatory paper holders (for flat packs or rolls) and towel rail brackets are made in either chromed metal or china : some of the metal ones are very neat and smooth with concealed fixings. Towel rails are not the most practical of objects. Even large heated ones are rarely large enough to hold individual towels for four or five members of a family, and they certainly won't hold them in a way which allows them to dry and look neat at the same time. So at least provide a small extra rail with clean dry towels for guests. A handsome but perfectly simple built-in towel rail is shown in the bathroom in fig 42. This would carry enough towels for a large family and their visitors, and it is ideally situated above the heating element.

Finally, be sure there are enough hooks on the door to take dressing gowns and hangers with clean clothes. It is infuriating, to say the least, if you like to dress in the bathroom before going out, as many women do, and are reduced to laying a freshly ironed dress on the floor.

Electrical installations

The combination of water and electricity is potentially lethal, so special care should be taken with electrical installations in a bathroom. In a brand new room, all this will automatically come within the scope of the architect or designer, but if it is a conversion job, which you are planning and possibly executing yourself, the following recommendations from the Institution of Electrical Engineers apply :

1 There should be no socket outlets, except, of course, specially fused razor sockets, and therefore no portable appliances.

2 A ceiling light should preferably be totally enclosed by the shade. If it is a pendant fitting, the flex should be covered in rubber and the bulb holder should be fitted with a rubber shield.

3 Switches in the room should be operated by a ceiling pull-cord.

4 Plugs specially designed to receive electric shavers are allowed.

Central heating is no longer considered un-
healthy (except by cranks), or even just the
prerogative of foreigners and rich men, and
many young people have no memories of
stepping from a hot bath into the steam-filled
chill of an unheated bathroom.

For the home where there is full central

45 Wall mirror conceals light fittings behind opalescent
strips; a shaver socket is mounted in the side panel.

heating, winter warmth in the bathroom is a
simple matter of an additional radiator, or, in the
case of blown warm-air heating, an additional
outlet grille. If you have, or intend to have, the

latter, make sure the grille is situated where it can provide not only general heat but a drying blast of warm air for the towel rail. Radiators, too, can perform this dual function if they are fitted with the type of towel rail specially designed for this purpose.

Unfortunately, plenty of homes still have no central heating. And anyway, what happens to those which do have it if the heating is turned off in the summer and the weather is cool? An oil-filled electric towel rail will take the chill off a very small room. But, of course, it must be left on permanently to do an adequate job— there is no question of flicking on the switch for a quick warm-up two minutes before you get in the bath. Instant heat *is* provided by infra-red heaters which should be fixed high up on a wall or ceiling, directed towards the area where most warmth is required and then fixed in position so that they do not need to be touched again. But these seem to me somewhat of an expedient: the bathroom is going to be chilly most of the time (which means all its surfaces will be chilly all the time), and it will positively invite streams of condensation. As a quick heat-boost for a bathroom which is normally centrally-heated, infra-red heaters have their uses though, and an extremely handsome one is now available which is ceiling fitted, thus giving the widest possible spread of heat, and is combined with a fluorescent light fitting.

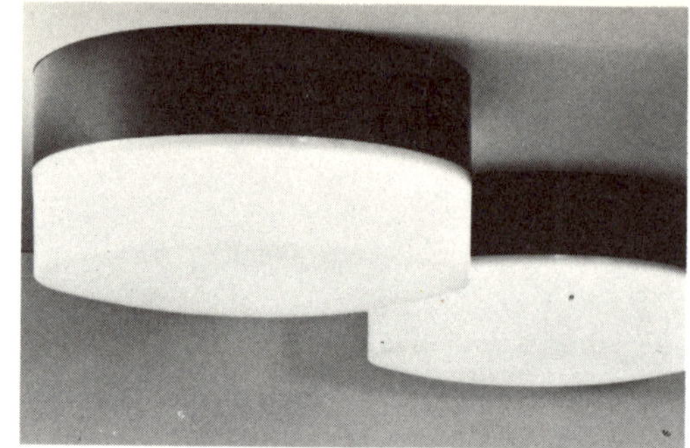

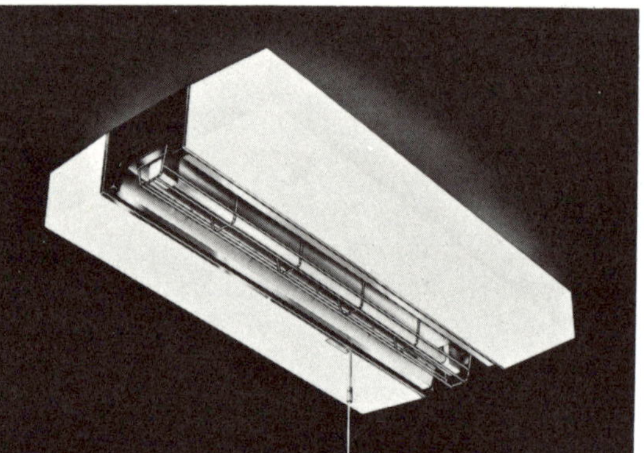

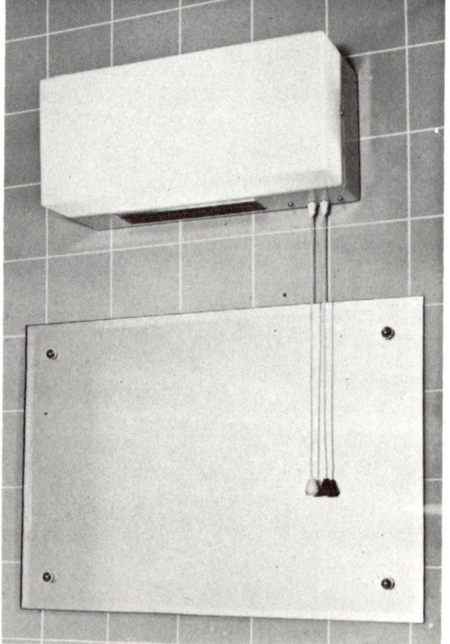

46a Trim light fittings with snap-on diffusers are ideal for bathroom use.
   b Ceiling-mounted radiant heater and light combined.
   c Fan heater and light combined.

A gentle background warmth, sufficient to ensure comfort in a small bathroom, comes from convector heaters (where cool air enters at the bottom, is drawn over the concealed heating element and passes out at the top to be re-circulated). And when a fan is incorporated, heat circulates more quickly to provide almost instant warmth. A small unit of this type is now on the market which has been combined with a light fitting consisting of two bulbs behind a plastic diffuser. Designed for wall mounting, say above a shaving mirror, it would provide very adequate heating for a small bathroom.

It hardly needs saying—but nevertheless I will—that free-standing electric fires with exposed elements are absolutely taboo in bathrooms. There should be no plug for them, of course, and I cringe at the memory of threading an electric-fire cord round a bath-room door and plugging it in on the landing. But I was a child and that was war-time, long before all the excellent and safe heating units which we enjoy now became available.

Water heating

In many houses water is heated by a boiler which also runs the central heating system. A new or additional bathroom can, in this case, probably tap the same source for its hot water supply, although you should check that the existing boiler is large enough to cope with the increased load. You may need a bigger one. But if there is no boiler, or if the new bathroom is too far away from the existing hot water supply to make an extension economic, you will need to install a local source of hot water. There are two main types: an instant hot water gas heater, or an electric water storage heater.

If a gas heater is mounted on an outside wall, it is a simple matter to install the necessary flue; but even when it is on an inside wall, the flue can generally be taken up through the joist space above the ceiling and so on to the exterior. All this must be considered at the planning stage. An electric water storage heater can, if necessary, be mounted directly above the bath—as with most other pieces of equipment nowadays, there are some with un-obtrusive, pared-down shapes—but most rooms still look prettier and better organized if the hot water proclaims its presence only when it gushes out of the tap. So if you can conceal the heater in an adjacent cupboard, recess or partition space, so much the better.

Lighting

When choosing lighting, it is worth remembering that a fluorescent tube gives about three times more light than a filament lamp and lasts about five times as long. So, although it costs more initially, it is in the long run less expensive. And with eight different shades of white to choose from, it is neither necessary nor sensible to end up with that cold, bleak look often associated with fluorescent lighting.

Lighting in a bathroom should, I think, be good and strong, unless you flinch at the slightest sign of a blemish or encroaching age. This is probably the one room in the house where there should be a fixed light which illuminates every corner. It doesn't have to be the only light, it doesn't have to be used by everyone, but it should be there for those who like to bath in a flood of light and see every speck of dust on the floor. It can take the form

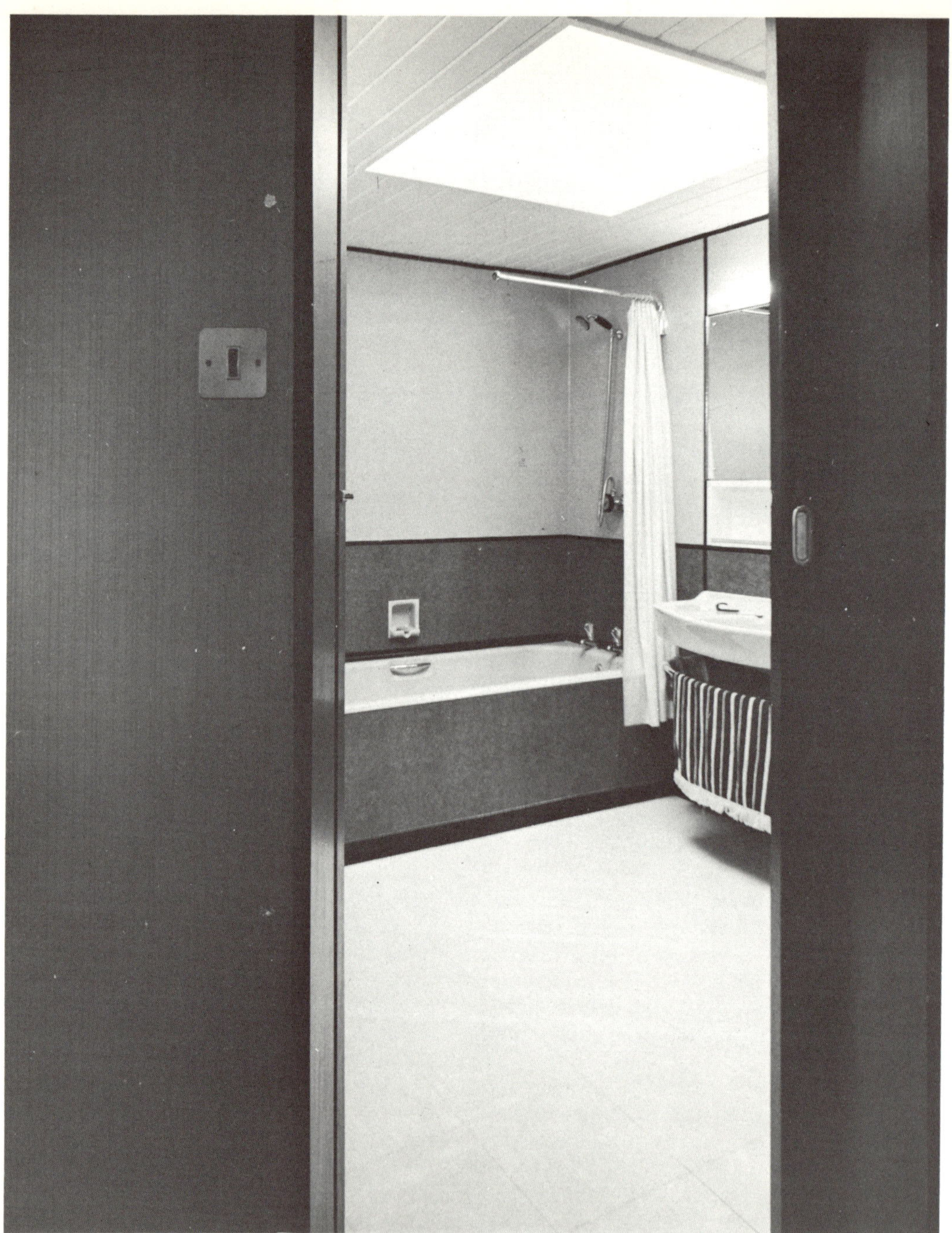

of a ceiling-mounted filament bulb fitting, or a suitably encased fluorescent tube, and, in the case of the former only, it can be operated by a dimmer switch, so that those who shrink from too much brightness can choose their own lower light level.

In addition, most people will probably want a separate mirror light for shaving and making up. This can be a spot or a fluorescent strip. An excellent bathroom mirror is made which incorporates lights. These shine through opalized panels in the mirror face, and a black vinyl strip down one side carries a shaver socket and a tooth-mug holder if required. The light given is soft (for the squeamish) but illuminating, and is operated by a pull switch. Strip lights with plastic diffuser shades, which also have a shaver socket set at one end, are a good alternative.

More esoteric lighting effects can be achieved in the bathroom as they can elsewhere in the house. High ceilings can be lowered with translucent plastic panels which conceal light fittings (there are many different types available), fluorescent strips can be concealed beneath shelves or wall-mounted cupboards to throw light on to working surfaces or washbowls below, lamps can be concealed behind plant troughs to throw the contents into sculptural relief. The number of fittings, from very narrow or circular fluorescent tubes to handsome and expensive lamps designed for filament bulbs, is large—the possibilities infinite.

Now that the advantages of conserving outside walls for living rooms, and placing other rooms in the centre of the house, have been realized, a bathroom no longer necessarily has daylight at all. If this is the case, the artificial lighting should be at a high level for daytime use, to avoid the depressing contrast which can be caused when passing from a brilliant sunlit bedroom to the comparative gloom of an underlit bathroom. However, many such bathrooms, particularly in modern houses or flat-roofed extensions, do have natural light from above in the form of a glass or plastic dome, which gives a pleasant pearly light as well as a view of sky and possibly trees.

If you have daylight which comes conventionally through a window, avoid a steel window frame unless you are completely convinced that you have the condensation

47 Architect Patrick Gwynne designed this bathroom which has a roof-light set in the wood-lined ceiling and walls and bath panel covered in fabric-backed vinyl.

49 Architect Edward Samuel designed his own bathroom so that all plumbing was concealed behind a partition; this space also houses cupboards and provides a mirror-backed shelf.

Opposite

48 Architect Anthony Cloughley's bathroom has walls lined in mulberry coloured felt, a stainless steel washbasin set in marble, with a stainless steel-covered plinth which conceals a dirty linen container.

problem beaten (it might rust), and do not be browbeaten by the risk of being seen from the next-door kitchen into having frosted glass, unless you really love it! Filmy Terylene curtains, reeded glass or translucent blinds are all more attractive alternatives. Only cross-reeded glass is really obscure though. All other types of so-called obscured glass are more or less revealing if you are standing close to them.

Ventilation

An extractor is obligatory in an internal bathroom (i.e. one with no window or natural ventilation) as this has to be mechanically ventilated, and it should be run off the same switch which operates the main light. When the light is switched on the extractor fan goes into action; after the light has been switched off an electrical relay allows the fan to go on functioning for a little longer. Extractor fans have a much wider application than this though. However hard you have worked at defeating the condensation problem with warmth, an extractor will whisk away any steam that does manage to form. And if you are at all fastidious and have a lavatory in the bathroom, you will want an extractor to remove unpleasant smells. Although not yet objects of beauty, most extractor fans are relatively unobtrusive and they can be fitted into the window, the wall or the ceiling. The wall does not have to be an external one because, again, the trunking can be carried through the joist space above to an outside wall. If you are not worried about steam extraction, there is an extractor fan which is fitted to the wc and removes unpleasant smells at source before they can penetrate to other parts of the house, a super refinement for those who have everything.

4 Storage

In a mini-bathroom, storage will necessarily be minimal too, although, as I have said elsewhere, it is essential that this sort of room should have some sort of receptacle for all the bathroom paraphernalia. A mirror-fronted cupboard would be suitable, but even better would be a vanitory unit with a really large low-level cupboard, tall enough to hold tins of cleaning powder, bottles of disinfectant, twin-masted schooners and the baby's pot. Lavatory brushes are hideous but essential implements and notoriously difficult to house. Many are sold with their own containers and sit coyly alongside the wc only to be knocked over by every passing toddler—and probably touched by him too! The most attractive I ever saw was reposing, solid and protected, in a rose-bedecked Victorian chamber-pot. Best of all, though, they should be put away out of sight, and, again, a tall cupboard beneath a vanitory unit would be a suitable place. There are several ready-made units on the market, but planners of a new bathroom will probably want to build their own, possibly running along the whole of one wall and incorporating their special requirements: drawers for cosmetics, separate compartments in the cupboard for toys, cleaning equipment and toilet articles, a working surface in laminated plastic, tiles or marble, and so on. Even a small room would take this type of fitting. A larger bathroom, especially one off a bedroom, may also be used as a dressing-room, with storage for clothes, and this is a perfectly satisfactory arrangement where there is warmth and no condensation. Sliding or folding-sliding doors which save space are particularly appropriate in this context.

The bathroom is the obvious place for housing surplus towels, and, if it is also to be used as a laundry room, it is a good site for the airing cupboard. This can have a small, individual heating element or be combined with a cupboard having a hot water storage tank, and share the warmth escaping from that. If you are building new cupboards in a bathroom, whether it is big or small, arrange them to improve its shape rather than the reverse. They can also do a specific job, such as forming a screen between lavatory and bath, or hiding ugly central heating trunking and water pipes.

Many bathrooms have room for a built-in dirty linen box, perhaps in the space between bath-end and wall or beneath a vanitory unit, and this is infinitely preferable to a basket or box cluttering up the floor space and hindering cleaning operations. Don't forget to provide some ventilation or it will smell.

Shelves can be good lavish ones, formed by window sills or by taking a concealing partition only halfway up a wall, or by making a recess in a partition wall. Lined with tiles or laminated plastic or hardwood, and possibly with concealed lighting, this sort of shelf provides a safe and decorative home for house plants (which flourish in a warm damp atmosphere), and any other handsome object you choose to beautify the room. Much less attractive are those narrow, ricketty-looking glass shelves with metal balustrades which are often placed above washbasins. They soon become the dumping ground for squeezed toothpaste tubes and empty shampoo bottles and acquire an added patina of dust, talcum powder and soap splashes. They take ages to clean and if you dismantle them in the process, they are inordinately easy to drop. Bathroom shelves should be wide, solid and cleaned with a quick wipe—or they should be banished.

50 The washbasin in Edward Samuel's bathroom is set in a wide useful shelf beneath the window.

51 Concealed plumbing partition provides a shelf along the whole length of one wall.

In a house where there are small children, any medicine kept in the bathroom should be housed in a locked cupboard, or, if you fear losing the key, in one which is fitted with a safety device which small fingers cannot operate. A reasonably good one has recently come on to the market.

5 Decoration

53 The lavish bathroom in a country house designed by architect Rodney Gordon. It has a view across the garden, a washbasin set in a peninsula unit and cork and wood-lined walls.

Opposite

52 Another view of Peter Moll's bathroom (see fig 43) showing bath boxed in in blockboard covered with marble-type vinyl tiles. These also form a curved dressing shelf and floor covering.

Walls

If you are old enough to associate bathrooms with white or grim green tiles and brown linoleum floors, forget your childhood memories. All those tiles made it easy to wipe away the streaming condensation, but in our splendid new bathrooms we shan't have any, so we can let rip with practically any material we fancy to decorate the walls.

The simplest and cheapest, if not the most exciting, is paint. And now, paint manufacturers having cottoned on to the fact that many of their customers actually want strong or subtle colours as well as the more everyday ones, this need not be nearly as dreary an exercise as it sounds. Emulsion paint is generally recommended for bathroom walls, because it has absorbent qualities and soaks up some of the steam. However, since, despite all claims to the contrary, its 'washable' qualities are disputable—you can certainly wash off patches of dirt, but you are left with terribly obtrusive patches of 'clean'—it is more sensible to paint the walls with a gloss or egg-shell finish paint, both of which are hard and tough and really do wipe clean. The condensation, if there is any, only sits on their surface. Softwood, which has to be painted, as opposed to any hardwood (boarding or shelves) which does not, should also be treated with a hard gloss for easy cleaning.

Painted walls are for many people only an inexpensive expedient or a last resort. Illustrated in this book, for instance, are bathroom walls covered in wood, felt, vinyl, laminated plastic, stainless steel and good old tiles. None of them shows signs of wearing or looking tatty. An extremely cheap form of decoration, costing very little more than paint in some cases, is a wallpaper with a plastic finish, which can be wiped clean and changed at little cost when it looks tired or you can't bear the sight of it any longer. Harder wearing would be a paper-backed vinyl, with which you can cover your walls in simulated marble, wood, Victorian flock, leopard skin or flowers—and a great many more things besides. It is available now in designs to suit every conceivable taste, it scrubs and is tough enough to stand normal wear and tear. Even tougher, and more expensive, are the fabric-backed vinyls which are completely impervious and will last almost as long as the bathroom.

Tiles can be in delicate pastel colours, or rich and sombre ones, they can be smooth or embossed, matt or gloss, patterned or plain, large or small, usually square and occasionally oblong. They no longer need look in any way clinical, though in many architect-designed bathrooms they frequently and intentionally do—as one architect explains: 'To me a bathroom is a workshop which should function perfectly in as little space as possible.' But for the unabashed sybarite there is colour and pattern in profusion.

Wood boarding, of which pine is the cheapest, set horizontally or vertically, makes a warm, colourful and very practical finish for bathroom walls. Treat it with matt button polish, so that it can be wiped clean, or varnish it if you like a high gloss. In either case you will find that it is astonishingly resistant to dirt and damage. A narrow, plate-glass splash-panel run along behind the washbasin would provide all the protection that is necessary.

The bathroom shown in fig 48 is lined entirely with a deep mulberry-coloured felt, to give a warm, svelte appearance, which is nevertheless perfectly hard-wearing. After months of use, it was unmarked and immaculate and contributed great style to a sophisticated, masculine setting.

The cool, hard appearance of laminated plastic makes it unattractive as a wall covering for some people, though it comes in a variety of brilliant colours and patterns (including mock wood). But the textured range developed for *QE2* has a three-dimensional quality and

54 Mosaic, laminated-plastic, wood and mirror glass are all used as cladding materials in this smooth town bathroom designed by architect Ted Levy.

is much warmer to the touch than the old, smooth laminates. It comes in five patterns and several muted colours at present, but special floral and paisley design versions were made for *QE2* and obviously textured laminates of this kind and many more will be on the market before long. Note, though, that they are only suitable for vertical application, and are not intended to be used as working surfaces.

Almost any of the above materials could be used to cover the bath panels, if these have not been bought with the bath, including the felt, if it were then overlaid with a sheet of toughened glass; mirror glass could be used too, especially if you wanted to obtain double value from an exceptionally attractive floor covering.

Floors

Because close carpeting is soft and warm, it has acquired luxury status in the bathroom, but it can be revoltingly unhygienic around a lavatory, especially if there are small boys in the family, and is likely to become sodden around the bath and washbasin. One designer lines the floor beneath with sheet polythene before laying wool carpets as a protection

55 The five textured laminated plastic designs which are now on the market.

against damp, but a synthetic carpet with a waterproof foam back is generally satisfactory and washes well. Those mats which are designed to sit like anguished frills round lavatory pedestals are among the nastier bathroom accessories, but since they are washable they are really essential when you have fitted carpet.

Any of the hard floor surfaces can be softened with washable cotton or nylon rugs, and these look well on ceramic tiles, mosaic, cork, vinyl or linoleum. An uncompromisingly hard cold surface such as ceramic tiles or mosaic is fine, if you have electric underfloor heating, but it tends to be noisy, especially if there are hard surfaces on the walls too, and is cold to the feet with other types of heating. Cork floors, especially now that they are obtainable with a water-resistant plastic finish, are quiet, warm and relatively soft on the feet. Coloured versions are not nearly as appealing as the natural shades which would be attractive in a simple, unpretentious bathroom, but probably too homely if you are striving for grandeur or sophistication. Linoleum, in sheet or tile form, certainly no longer has the bleak connotations of the past and comes in a number of splendid colours but it cannot offer the exotic patterns produced by the vinyl tile manufacturers. Pure colours, marble, mosaic, wood-blocks, cobble stones, French faience tiling are only a few of the affects that can be achieved with vinyl tiling, and many of them look a good deal better than they probably sound. They are easily washable, warmish to the touch and no more slippery when wet than linoleum or tiles. Incidentally, a rug is useful in a bathroom for its anti-slip as well as its comfort-promoting properties.

Colour

It is impossible not to be subjective about colour. We all have highly personal, often idiosyncratic views, from the aesthetic architect for whom colour in the bathroom means white, natural wood and possibly cork, to the cheerful sybarite who can produce a room which is both attractive and unusual with a riotous combination of colours. Then there are all the others in between: those who have a genius for putting the right colours together in exactly the wrong hideous combination; those who play safe and have everything matching; those who stick to pastel shades; those who mix patterns, those who don't, those who cannot bear strong colours first thing in the morning, those who think dark colours are masculine in appearance, those who think women's complexions are flattered by pink . . . . Most of us, rightly or wrongly, are perfectly happy with our colour rules and it would be presumptuous to try to impose others.

In the past the main argument against coloured sanitary ware was that it cost more. It cost 25 per cent more initially, and it meant that you were tied to one colour scheme for the rest of its natural life, unless you were rich enough to replace it when you wanted a change of scene. Now all this has changed. With the advent of acrylic (Perspex) baths and bowls, you can have a colour for the same price as white, so the initial outlay is no more. But the same problem arises when you come to change your colour scheme. And if you have a flaming orange bath (which you can in acrylic), you are likely to want to change it rather sooner than if you started off with a less flamboyant colour. Remember, too, that lavatories and bidets do not come in the same material, so you cannot have a matching set! Matching is a problem, whatever material you choose, since many manufacturers do not make every item of sanitary ware. For instance, in the bathroom shown in fig 53, the lavatory, bidet and wash-basin are in a deep petrol-blue, but as the manufacturer of these items did not make baths, the owners were reduced to buying the steel shell of a bath elsewhere and having it sprayed to their exact colour requirements at the local garage.

Incidentally, in fairness to the manufacturers of traditional sanitary ware, it should be pointed out that their colours now include some soft, subtle shades which are a great deal more interesting than all those maidenly pastels with which they are usually associated. But really singing colour is still limited to acrylic sanitary ware, and to glass fibre goods, whose main *raison d'être* is that they are easily made in a profusion of colours and patterns.

Window dressing

In a bathroom which has been converted from a room in an old house the windows may be large and gracious. In a first class modern house set in its own grounds (which is just about the most uncommon type of property there is in England), the bathroom windows will probably have been designed to afford a beautiful view, as in the one in fig 53. Elsewhere they are likely to be small, utilitarian and, alas, ugly. The kind of dressing they receive will depend upon the owner's particular taste. For instance, the purist architect is unlikely to be a willing accomplice to frilly curtains, nor would they look good in his brand of bathroom. The owner of this type of neat, chic, no-nonsense bathroom would possibly plump for blinds. The roller blind may be a relic from our Victorian forbears, but in its light, updated version, with easily washable, plastic-treated surfaces, it is a simple and suitable fitting for a modern bathroom. Available in plain colours or some surprisingly good patterns, it is also possible to have them made up in your own fabric, although this, of course, is more expensive.

Venetian blinds, those other Victorian relics, are much less suitable for bathroom use, despite the fact that they can be used to filter light and regulate privacy, because they are dust traps of the first order. Admittedly the whole contraption, now made in plastic, can be taken down and dunked in a bath of hot soapy water, but this is not an easy or quick operation, nor is it one which many people enjoy. However, in the bathroom in fig 53 Venetian blinds have been set between the two skins of a double-glazed window where they do an excellent job and are protected from dust.

An immaculately neat idea is the hinged opal perspex screen which closes over the small

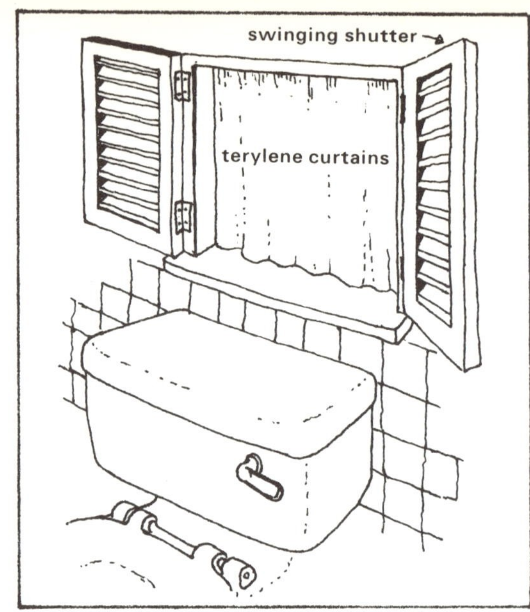

56 Terylene curtains provide privacy during the day, wooden shutters at night, in this basement bathroom.

window in the bathroom in fig 1. Easily cleaned, it obscures no light and would be a good solution in a bathroom with privacy problems.

Curtains, whether frilly or tailored, have a softening effect which will appeal to many people. This advantage is not only visual; it also has acoustic value in a room where there are bound to be a number of hard surfaces. Material? Anything you like, particularly where there is little condensation, although the traditional, easily-laundered cotton or towelling are probably more sensible if your family is likely to tug the curtains apart with soapy hands, or splatter them with liquid shampoo. An attractive, though not particularly cheap, arrangement I saw in the bathroom of a basement flat consisted of Terylene curtains which gave privacy during the day, with wooden louvred shutters closing at night.

6 For the future?

The post-war developments in plastics have probably had as much impact on bathrooms as on any other room in the house, with plastic floor and wall surfaces, colourful plastic sanitary ware, plastic plumbing pipes, plastic light fittings, roof lights and so on. But in every case, the actual item being manufactured in plastic was not new; in other words, it was an old piece of equipment made in a new material, sometimes for the better, sometimes not. Rarely has the full potential of a plastic material been exploited to the extent its unique properties merit. The moulding of glass fibre bonded resins into components which fit together to form a complete bathroom (as described on page 31) seems to be one of the few exceptions; and there are firms and individuals making timid sorties into the market for this sort of prefabricated bathroom in many different countries. These moulded bathrooms with their curved, easily cleaned surfaces, seem a neat package solution to the various problems of bathroom design, especially for mass housing. The fact that they are not sweeping the market means that they are probably not quite tough enough to measure up to the standards normally demanded for local authority housing; and they certainly do not look conventional enough for the speculative builder, always wary of consumer resistance to new ideas which will slow up his sales rate. Even architects, who, after all, are responsible for specifying what goes into housing developments, have not leapt into the vanguard with this particular product. Nevertheless, it is a development which seems to promise bathrooms of the future (even if it is only the distant future), which will be completely different in appearance and performance, the sort of bathroom which Gio Ponti, the eminent Italian architect describes as 'functionally perfect, orderly, sanitary, and easily maintained. This much is in good taste, nothing more.'

Meanwhile we are left with our traditional bathrooms, wherein I feel there remains fairly wide scope for improvement. Standards of design in individual items fluctuate wildly. Some are poor, some are extremely good, and many of the latter have been mentioned in this book. But there are still weak spots, which are common to most manufacturers and which, since they are remarked upon by many bathroom users, could surely be improved.

Difficulty in cleaning is one, with the lavatory probably the main offender. Some manufacturers have managed to simplify the shape, and done away with filth-collecting nooks and bends, and the cantilevered models certainly make for easier external cleaning. But would it not be possible to banish the dripping lavatory brush for ever by incorporating a built-in dispenser of strong cleansing fluid which operates each time the lavatory is flushed? And is there no means of attaching a lavatory seat to the wc itself without those tortured little hinges which are almost impossible to clean?

Lavatories are getting lower, which is, we are told, an aid to defecation. This will, I presume, increase the splashing which results from male urination, and is already a hygiene problem—especially for those who do the cleaning! The answer to that one seems to be some sort of neat male urinal for domestic installation—in which case fitted carpet in the bathroom would immediately become a much more hygienic proposition.

Well-designed baths are not particularly difficult to clean, as long as you are able to bend double, although the largest have to be tackled from within rather than from without. But shower trays demand that you get down on all fours, preferably naked because if there is a fixed shower rose, the water will gush all over you the minute you turn the tap on. There should, ideally, be a separate, adjustable hand shower for cleaning.

Although some taps and shower fittings are simple and relatively easily cleaned the majority are not, and their shape is another problem for industrial designers in the future. Foot control of water supply is not an especially attractive idea, since the 'controller' is often operating with bare feet, but lavatory flushing is another matter. Not only is it a much swifter and less fiddly action, there are good hygiene reasons for preferring to use the foot rather than the hand. Yet even the most thoughtfully planned bathrooms rarely have this refinement.

Noise from the bathroom which penetrates to the rest of the house is a frequent cause of annoyance, disturbance and embarrassment. Even syphonic lavatories are not exactly silent, poor plumbing results in gurgling pipes and human noises are unavoidable. So we may hope for even quieter lavatories in the future, improved plumbing which will not bang throughout the reaches of the night—and acoustic insulation which should take care of the rest. For instance, the fine modern bathroom in fig 1 has a layer of cork beneath the tiles which serves as both acoustic and thermal insulation. A lobby, perhaps containing storage and airing cupboards, would provide a literal sound barrier if there is space available.

Drainage pipes are not beautiful objects. Is it too much to ask that in future bathrooms they should always be concealed? This is not a particularly difficult or expensive operation, the most advanced washbasin manufacturers are already tucking theirs away within the bowels of the bowl, yet hundreds of new bathrooms still have their pipes on view, particularly in some of the poorer quality speculative estates. One country bathroom I know of is a riot of ancient pipes and trunking; it has been painstakingly papered by its owner so that every pipe is concealed beneath a layer of paper. The paper is pretty, this is an amusing expedient and the pipes have receded. But God forbid that it should ever be necessary in a modern bathroom.

Nobody has solved the problem of jointing yet, either. Whatever is used to fill the tiny gap between the bath and wall or washbasin and wall, it invariably cracks, crumbles or breaks away under the strain of cleaning and wetting. Can we expect a solution to this one in the future? Let us have some decent sized towel rails too, so that our towels can be spread out to dry even if we are six in a family. And why not some sort of inexpensive domestically-scaled disposal unit for bathroom garbage?

These are complaints and suggestions about things which are wrong. There is, however, a great deal that is right, many bathrooms are a pleasure to look at and to use.

The well-designed baths, washbasins etc. are there for those who choose carefully. The good architects and designers are available for those who believe planning is important and are prepared to pay for the best advice. The accessories, the surfaces, the equipment which makes a really first-rate and comfortable bathroom, can all be found in England as well as abroad. I hope this book will at least have served to point out some of the good things that are available and stimulated readers' interest sufficiently to make them search for the rest.

7 Government grants

Alterations, repairs and additions to a house are expensive, but the government, in its keenness to encourage the improvement of old properties, has made two types of grant available to anyone embarking on this sort of exercise: they are standard grants and discretionary grants. Before I describe these, let me warn you that no money can be granted once work has commenced. You must apply to your local authority in writing and get their written offer of a grant before you lift a brick. Anyone is eligible for a grant, and no means test is applied.

Standard grants

These are made by local councils to people who want to provide a house or flat for the first time with:

a	fixed bath or shower	£25
b	washbasin	£5
c	hot and cold water at washbasin	£35
	hot and cold water at bath	£15
	hot and cold water at sink	£25
d	inside lavatory	£40
e	larder	£10

I have shown the maximum grant available. You may, for instance, already have a larder and a lavatory and only need the first five items, in which case you would be eligible for a maximum of £105; if you need all seven items, you would be eligible for the maximum of £155. You can in fact apply for half the cost of improvements, within this £155 maximum, if the house was built before 1945 or was converted before October 1951 from a property built before 1945. But the local council must be satisfied that when the work has been done the house will be habitable for another fifteen years. Since we are here principally concerned with bathrooms, it should be pointed out that if a bathroom can only be provided by building on or converting outbuildings *or* if you need a septic tank drainage for your new lavatory *or* if you are bringing piped cold water into the house for the first time, then the grant is subject to a maximum of £350 instead of the normal £155.

Discretionary grants

These are not so directly applicable to bathrooms, but are available from local councils to help owners bring houses up to a good standard generally, or to convert large old houses into flats. If you are embarking on a large scale project which includes but goes beyond providing a bathroom, do consult the local authority first. Councils have discretion to pay up to one half the estimated cost of the work (including professional fees) as approved by them, up to a maximum of £400 per house improved or per flat produced by conversion—and this rises to £500 per flat in larger houses.* The council needs to be satisfied that the house will have a life of thirty years after the work is done. If you are worried about finding the remaining half of the cost, consult your mortgage society, who may be prepared to extend their loan.

There are certain perfectly fair restrictions attached to these loans. You may let a house or flat which has been converted with the aid of council money, but if you sell it within three years to anyone outside your own family, part of the loan will have to be repayed. There are also certain rent restrictions on properties you propose to let. But full details and advice can be obtained from your own local authority who—may I repeat!—should be consulted long before the work is started.

---

* All figures were correct at the time of going to press, but changes were imminent.

Sanitary Ware

Adamsez Ltd, Artillery Mansions, 76 Victoria Street, London SW1 (*not baths*)

Allied Ironfounders Ltd, 28 Brook Street, London W1 (*baths, bowls and shower cubicles only*)

Armitage Ware Ltd, 303-6 High Holborn, London WC1

Geoffrey Bonsack Ltd, 14 Mount Street, London W1 (*glassfibre baths and bowls*)

Carron, Hancock Road, London E3 (*baths and bowls*)

Fordham Pressings Ltd, Dudley Road, Wolverhampton (*lavatories and cisterns*)

Glass Fibre Laminates Ltd, White Lund, Morecambe, Lancashire. (*baths and shower cubicles only*)

Alfred Goslett & Co Ltd, Charing Cross Road, WC2

Wm. Heaton & Co Ltd, Millmoor Works, Rotheram (*baths only*)

Ideal Standard Ltd, Ideal House, Great Marlborough St, London W1

Harold Moore & Son Ltd, Bailey Works, Bailey Street, Panel X Plastics Ltd, Cirencester, Gloucestershire (*baths only*)

Sheffield (*baths, shower trays and vanitory units*)

Shanks & Co Ltd, 18 North Audley Street, London W1

Shires Ltd, 5a Berners Street, London W1

John Steventon & Sons Ltd, Royal Venton Works, Middlewich, Cheshire

Twyfords Ltd, Stoke-on-Trent, Staffordshire (*not baths*)

Shower cubicles

Allied Ironfounders Ltd, 28 Brook Street, London W1

Armitage Plastics Ltd, 303-6 High Holborn, London WC1

Dahl Brothers Ltd, 22 Replingham Road, London SW18

Gardex Ltd, Bredbury, Stockport, Cheshire

Glass Fibre Laminates Ltd, White Lund, Morecambe, Lancashire

H. L. Kinns Ltd, Shere, Surrey

Seaflow Manufacturing Co Ltd, 6 Brantwood Road, Luton, Bedfordshire

Taps and shower fittings

Adamsez Ltd, Artillery Mansions, 76 Victoria Street, London SW1

Armitage Ware Ltd, 303-6 High Holborn, London WC1

Barber Wilsons & Co Ltd, Crawley Road, Wood Green, London N22

Barking Brassware Co Ltd, River Road, Barking, Essex

James Barwell Ltd, Great Hampton Street, Birmingham 18

Belco, Belco House, Park Royal Road, London NW10

F. H. Bourner & Co Ltd, Manor Royal, Crawley, Sussex

IMI Developments Ltd, PO Box 216, Birmingham 6

Meynell & Sons Ltd, Montrose Street, Wolverhampton

Sanbra Ltd, 8-9 Clerkenwell Green, London EC1

Walker Crosweller & Co Ltd, Cheltenham, Gloucestershire

Wall and floor coverings

Amtico Flooring Ltd, Celanese House, Hanover Square, London W1 (*vinyl tiles*)

Formica Ltd, De La Rue House, Regent Street, London W1

H. & R. Johnson Ltd, Stoke-on-Trent (*ceramic tiles and mosaic*)

Nairn Coated Products, 6 Cranford Way, Tottenham Lane, Hornsey, London (*vinyl tiles, vinyl coated paper and fabric*)

Pearson Lightweight Mirror Co, 92 West Bar, Sheffield

Pilkingtons, St Helen's, Lancashire (*mirror glass*)

Pilkington and Carter, 42 Bloomsbury Street, London WC1 (*ceramic tiles and mosaic*)

Storeys of Lancaster, White Cross, Lancaster (*paper-backed vinyl*)

Warerite, 12 Grosvenor Gardens, London SW1

Wicanders (Great Britain) Ltd, Maxwell Road, Crawley, Sussex (*cork tiles*)

Heaters

Dimplex Ltd, 580 Purley Way, Croydon, Surrey

Denham & Morley Ltd, Denmore House, 173 Cleveland Street, London W1

Electrolux Ltd, Luton, Bedfordshire

Saltire Electric Ltd, Powder Mill Lane, Dartford, Kent

Sterling Domestic Appliances, Sterling Works, Dagenham, Essex

Extractors

Silavent Ltd, 32 Blyth Road, Hayes, Middlesex

Vent Axia, 60 Rochester Row, SW1

Xpelair, PO Box 15, Colchester, Essex

Water heaters

Ascot Gas Water Heaters Ltd, 59 Baker Street, London W1

Associated Electrical Industries, 33 Grosvenor Place, London SW1

Heatrae Ltd, Norwich, Norfolk

Sadia Water Heaters Ltd, Northolt, Middlesex

Santon Ltd, Santon House, Old Oak Common Lane, Acton, London W3

Prefabricated bathrooms

Finlock Products Ltd, Penmill Trading Estate Yeovil, Somerset
Fulboro, 71 St Albans Road, Hatfield, Hertfordshire
Planimac Ltd, Station House, Darkes Lane, Potters Bar, Hertfordshire
Surface Productions Ltd, Adelaide House, King William Street, London EC4

Accessories

G. & S. Allgood Ltd, Carterville House, 297 Euston Road, London NW1 (*architectural ironmongery including two-way locks, toilet roll holders, soap dishes etc.*)
H. & R. Johnson Ltd, Stoke-on-Trent, (*ceramic soap dishes etc.*)
Limpitt & Co (Aldridge) Ltd, 131 Mill Green, Aldridge, Staffordshire (*magnetic soap holder*)
Merchant Adventurers Ltd, Interlight House, Feltham, Middlesex (*light fittings*)
Metlex Industries Ltd, Sumner Road, Croydon (*mirrors, toilet roll holders, towel rails etc.*)
Pilkington and Carter, 42 Bloomsbury Street, London WC1 (*ceramic soap dishes etc.*)
Sundaw Products Ltd, 109 Union Street, Smethwick, Worcestershire (*architectural ironmongery including two-way locks*)

Acknowledgements

for addresses see under Manufacturers
Photographers
Richard Einzig figs 14, 24, 54; Desmond O'Neill figs 6, 12, 43, 44, 48, 52; Sam Lambert figs 5, 53; Stella Samuel figs 23, 49, 50; Henk Snoek fig 47.

1	Adamsez bathroom fittings
8	Lock from Sundaw Products Ltd
10	Textured laminate by Formica Ltd
15b	Dahl Brothers Ltd
16a	H. L. Kinns Ltd; **b** Allied Ironfounders Ltd
17a, b	Walker Crosweller & Co Ltd
18	F. H. Bourner & Co
19	Wm. Heaton & Co
21	Surface Productions Ltd
22	Geoffrey Bonsack Ltd
25	Carron
26a	Ideal Standard Ltd; **b** Allied Ironfounders Ltd
27a	Glass Fibre Laminates Ltd; **b** Allied Ironfounders Ltd; **c** Ideal Standard Ltd; **d** Carron; **e** Geoffrey Bonsack
28a, b	Armitage Ware Ltd; **c** Carron; **d** Alfred Goslett & Co
29	Twyfords Ltd
30a	Shanks & Co; **b** Twyfords Ltd; **c** Adamsez Ltd
31a, b	Ideal Standard Ltd
32a	Ideal Standard Ltd; **b** Shires Ltd; **c** Adamsez Ltd; **d** Shanks & Co; **e** Shires Ltd
33a	Armitage Ware Ltd; **b, c** Fordham Pressings Ltd
34a, b	Armitage Ware Ltd; **c** Adamsez Ltd; **d** Shanks & Co
35, 36	Walker Crosweller & Co
37a	Adamsez Ltd; **b** Shanks & Co
39a,	**b** Armitage Ware Ltd
40a	Shanks & Co; **b** IMI Developments Ltd; **c** Adamsez Ltd
41	Limpitt & Co
45	Metlex Industries Ltd
46a	Merchant Adventurers Ltd; **b** Saltire Electric Ltd; **c** Dimplex Ltd
55	Formica Ltd